Developing Citizenship in the Curriculum

Edited by Janet Edwards
and
Ken Fogelman

David Fulton Publishers

London

David Fulton Publishers Ltd
2 Barbon Close, London WC1N 3JX

First published in Great Britain by
David Fulton Publishers 1993

Note: The right of the authors to be identified as the authors of this work has been asserted by them
in accordance with the copyright, Designs and Patents Act 1988.

Copyright © David Fulton Publishers Ltd

British Library Cataloguing in Publication Data

A catalogue record for this book is available from the British Library

ISBN 1-85346-224-6

Typeset by Textype Typesetters, Cambridge
Printed in Great Britain by BPCC Wheaton Ltd, Exeter

Developing Citizenship in the
Curriculum

for return on or before the

Contents

Contributors

RICHARD APLIN	Lecturer in Education, University of Leicester
PATRICK BAILEY	Consultant in Education and Trustee of the Geographical Association
TERRY BROWN	Advisory Teacher for Health Education, Northamptonshire LEA
MAX BUCZYNSKI	Head of Economics and Business Studies, Prince William School, Oundle
MAX BURKIMSHER	Deputy Head, Guilsborough School, Northamptonshire
FRANK CONLEY	General Secretary, The Politics Association and Head of Politics at the Harvey Grammar School, Folkestone
IAN DUFFELL	Industrial Fellow, Centre for Citizenship Studies in Education, University of Leicester
JANET EDWARDS	Deputy Director, Centre for Citizenship Studies in Education, University of Leicester
JANICE FELCE	Advisory Teacher and SCIP Coordinator, Northamptonshire LEA
KEN FOGELMAN	Director, Centre for Citizenship Studies in Education and Professor of Education, University of Leicester
STEVE GOODALL	Headteacher, Old Stratford County Primary School, Northamptonshire
ROSE GRIFFITHS	Lecturer in Education, University of Leicester
LINDA HARGREAVES	Lecturer in Education, University of Leicester
JENNY HARRISON	Lecturer in Education, University of Leicester
SUE HARRISON	Chief Adviser, Education Department, Leicestershire LEA
TINA JARVIS	Lecturer in Education, University of Leicester
CHRIS JONES	Development Officer, Community Education Development Centre, Coventry
DAVID KERR	Lecturer in Education, University of Leicester

NEIL KITSON	Lecturer in Education, University of Leicester
GEORGE KNIGHTS	General Adviser, Education Department, Leicestershire LEA
TONY LAWSON	Lecturer in Education, University of Leicester
MARK LOFTHOUSE	Senior Lecturer in Education, University of Leicester
ROS MCCULLOCH	Lecturer in Education, University of Leicester
JOHN POTTER	Manager, Community Service Volunteers in Education, London N1
GRAHAM ROBB	Headteacher, Lode Heath School, Solihull
PATRICIA ROGERS	Head, Council for Education in World Citizenship, London W1
DON ROWE	Director of The Citizenship Foundation, London EC1
ADRIAN STOKES	Lecturer in Education, University of Leicester
GORDON VINCENT	County Adviser, Education Department, Buckinghamshire LEA
MARTIN WENHAM	Lecturer in Education, University of Leicester
ANGELA WORTLEY	Lecturer in Education, University of Leicester

CHAPTER 1

Introduction – *Developing Citizenship in the Curriculum*

Janet Edwards and Ken Fogelman

This book is the second collection of writings on education for citizenship produced by the Centre for Citizenship Studies in Education, University of Leicester. The first book (Fogelman, 1991), which was written before the publication of the NCC guidance on citizenship education, was based in part on research carried out for the Speaker's Commission on Citizenship, and also contained accounts of philosophies, approaches and activities by individual schools and education authorities.

In the past two years, it has become apparent that a major challenge for schools is to integrate the cross-curricular themes into the curriculum. What is their relevance to the specialist subject teacher? How can the hard-pressed primary teacher ensure their coverage alongside the statutory programmes of study and statements of attainment? How does a school ensure that each student's experience makes sense – across the curriculum at any one time, and over time?

It is such questions that this book attempts to begin to address. However, the first part of this introductory chapter provides a summary of the guidance which has appeared in the last two years, mainly emanating from the National Curriculum Council.

Published Guidance

Consideration of recent developments in education for citizenship begins with a fundamental statement from the 1988 Education Reform Act, which placed a statutory responsibility upon schools to provide a broad and balanced curriculum which '*promotes the spiritual, moral, cultural, mental and physical development of pupils at the school and of society*' and '*prepares pupils for the opportunities and experiences of adult life.*'

More specific reference appeared in *Curriculum Guidance 3: The Whole*

Curriculum (NCC 1990), which set the context for developing the school curriculum and explained that the 'basic curriculum' (core and foundation subjects and RE) can form the foundation but will not, on its own, provide the necessary breadth. It should be 'augmented by additional subjects, an accepted range of cross-curricular elements and extra-curricular activities'. In addition there will be 'intangibles which come from the spirit and ethos of each school, its pupils and staff, teaching methods, management of the curriculum and of the school.'

Cross-curricular elements were described as:

- **dimensions** – which give equality of opportunity to all pupils, and take account of diversity of gender, cultural and linguistic background, and special educational needs.

- **skills** – communication;
  – numeracy;
  – study;
  – problem solving;
  – personal and social;
  – information technology.

- **themes** – Economic and Industrial Understanding;
  – Careers Education and Guidance;
  – Health Education;
  – Education for Citizenship;
  – Environmental Education.

In the same document, the aims of education for citizenship were described as being to:

- *establish the importance of positive, participative citizenship and provide the motivation to join in;*
- *help pupils to acquire and understand essential information on which to base the development of their skills, values and attitudes towards citizenship.*

Guidance 3 was followed by five further documents, one on each of the themes. Number 8, *Education for Citizenship* contains this statement, which may serve as a starting point for a school's discussion and development of its own policy:

> Education for Citizenship develops the knowledge, skills and attitudes necessary for exploring, making informed decisions about and exercising responsibilities and rights in a democratic society.

In the same document, objectives for education for citizenship are categorised as knowledge, cross-curricular skills, attitudes, moral codes and values.

Eight essential Components for study (and areas within each of these) are identified, and these may be seen as a suggested curriculum outline for education for citizenship.

The *components* are:

- Community;
- Pluralist Society;
- Being a Citizen;
- Family;
- Democracy;
- Citizen and Law;
- Work, Employment and Leisure;
- Public Services.

Activities (tasks, opportunities and experiences) which will promote the personal development of pupils, encourage them to develop caring attitudes and a desire to participate in events happening in the world about them are also suggested. The ethos of a school can do much to support these activities and education for citizenship is likely to be most successful in schools which encourage equality of opportunity, community links, mutual respect, pupil autonomy and responsibility, group and extra-curricular activities and active involvement of pupils in lessons. These and many other aspects of school life can, together, demonstrate that citizenship is not simply a body of knowledge, but is embedded in all that a school is and does. However, without an appropriate knowledge base, wise and informed decisions cannot be made or appropriate systems developed to encourage participation.

The Speaker's Commission on Citizenship

A further valuable contribution to the debate can be found in *Encouraging Citizenship* (HMSO,1990), the report of the Speaker's Commission on Citizenship. It identified the study of citizenship as involving:

- understanding the rules;
- the acquisition of knowledge;
- the development and exercise of skills;
- learning democratic behaviour through the experience of the school as a community, and from the experience of the school as an institution playing a role in the wider community.

The Commission stresses that the opportunity for learning provided by community experiences will provide an indispensable springboard to encourage students to make a voluntary contribution in later life. The report identifies skills, both intellectual and social, which are necessary to understand and address issues of rights and responsibilities.

- **Intellectual skills** include:
  - skills associated with written and oral expression;
  - skills involving judgement;
  - the identification of bias, prejudice, stereotypes and discrimination.

- **Social skills** include:
  - recognising and accepting differences;
  - establishing positive and non-oppressive personal relationships;
  - resolving conflict in a non-violent way;
  - taking responsibility;
  - participating in decisions.

This report has much in common with the NCC guidance, and together they can be seen as:

  - encouragement to go beyond the statutory requirements of the National Curriculum and establish whole school policies for Citizenship Education;
  - an agenda for debate in the community of each school – with pupils, teachers, parents and governors – for moving ahead in partnership for positive participative Citizenship.

Citizenship in the Curriculum

Coherence in the curriculum was one of the principles upon which the Education Reform Act was based. However, the way in which the subject and cross-curricular documents emerged from the National Curriculum Council lacked coherence. There is a risk that pupils will see their learning as a series of discrete experiences unless teachers and community partners work together to make sense of the curriculum jig-saw (see, for example, Hargreaves, 1991). There is a real opportunity to use the cross-curricular elements as a constructive way forward towards ensuring entitlement and coherence in the learning experiences of all pupils.

The National Curriculum Council did not follow the Curriculum Guidance documents with any INSET advice for whole curriculum planning and we are aware that without such guidance the task is sometimes perceived by schools as almost too difficult to contemplate. The NCC has produced working papers entitled 'Setting the scene: commonality in the cross-curricular themes', 'Overview of the cross-curricular themes' and 'Equal opportunities and ERA' (March 1992). In addition, there have been some publications, in journals during 1992, focusing on interpretations of citizenship and the implications for the school curriculum (examples include special editions of *The Journal of Moral Education* (Vol **21** No. 3) and of *International Studies in Sociology of Education* (Vol **2** No 1)).

Publications addressing the issues of integration and coherence across the whole curriculum are rare, but include INSET packs being prepared for publication by the Centre for Citizenship Studies in Education, due to appear at the same time as this book (Edwards and Pathan 1993).

If the cross-curricular elements are to permeate the curriculum an essential pre-requisite seems to us to be that those responsible for the implementation of the core and foundation subjects should consider the relationship between their own subjects and the themes. This book aims to facilitate the understanding of Education for Citizenship and its relationship with other curriculum areas. Written as it is by those with special knowledge of, and experience in, areas of the curriculum other than citizenship it presents a unique collection of writings. It should be of interest to subject teachers in schools, to those involved in Initial Teacher Training, as well as to all those acting in advisory capacities or pursuing research.

Chapter 2 summarises some of the issues that arose at a conference in Northamptonshire in May 1991. The teachers, advisers and other educationalists present were interested in the management issues for schools trying to implement cross-curricular learning. Discussion of ethos, self-esteem, curriculum planning and community partnerships raised much interest. In Chapter 3 the planning process is addressed and the authors draw on work with Leicestershire teachers in all phases. Suggestions for curriculum mapping are described. Chapter 4 brings together short sections on the relationships seen to exist among the five themes, which certainly should not be seen as discrete from one another. Chapter 5 is the place where subject specialists, drawn from our colleagues at the University of Leicester School of Education, look at citizenship. These contributions have brought particular interest to the editors. It has been stimulating and helpful to us to have so much wide-ranging experience brought to bear upon our own special area of interest and we are extremely grateful to them. We trust that there will also be a bonus for the cross-curricular aspects of the Initial Teacher Training course at Leicester!

The title of Chapter 6 has been the subject of some debate. Some of the subject areas represented there might be those whose practitioners and supporters feel to be marginalised by the National Curriculum. It is certainly not our intention to add to this feeling by including them in a varied collection of contributions at the end of the book. On the contrary, each area is seen as important in its own right and in its contribution to citizenship education. Indeed with a topic as wide as citizenship it is not difficult to think of additional areas – such as multi-cultural education and special educational needs – which would have a case for inclusion.

Our hope is that the pieces gathered here will be of interest to all practitioners, and help them to acknowledge the relevance of their own specialism. Our ambition is that no teacher will want to claim that education for citizenship is someone else's responsibility.

References

Edwards, J. (1993) *Citizenship*. Cambridge: Pearson.

Edwards, J. and Pathan, L. *Cross-curricular INSET and Resources*. Cambridge: Pearson.

Fogelman, K. (ed.) (1991) *Citizenship in Schools*. London: Fulton.

Hargreaves, D. (1991) 'Coherence and Manageability: reflections on the National Curriculum and cross-curricular provision' *The Curriculum Journal* 2 (1).

6

Reference to the following documents occurs repeatedly in the text. They are referred to here in full but will not be so listed as they are mentioned in subsequent pages. Abbreviated references will be given as for example *NCC(1990f)* or *Curriculum Guidance 8*.

National Curriculum Council (1990a) *Curriculum Guidance 3: The Whole Curriculum*. York: NCC.

National Curriculum Council (1990b) *Curriculum Guidance 4: Economic and Industrial Understanding*. York: NCC.

National Curriculum Council (1990c) *Curriculum Guidance 5: Health Education*. York: NCC.

National Curriculum Council (1990d) *Curriculum Guidance 6: Careers Education and Guidance*. York: NCC.

National Curriculum Council (1990e) *Curriculum Guidance 7: Environmental Education*. York: NCC.

National Curriculum Council (1990f) *Curriculum Guidance 8: Education for Citizenship*. York: NCC.

Speaker's Commission on Citizenship (1990) *Encouraging Citizenship*. London: HMSO.

CHAPTER 2

Creating a Climate for Citizenship Education in Schools

Max Burkimsher

This chapter is a synthesis of discussion which took place at the inaugural conference of the Centre for Citizenship Studies in Education, in May 1991. On that occasion participants, from schools and local authorities throughout England, considered issues relating to the readiness of schools for citizenship education in the light of recently published guidance from the National Curriculum Council and the report of the Speakers' Commission on Citizenship (1990).

There emerged considerable unanimity about the nature of citizenship education, the activities and experiences which contribute to it and a vision of what it might become. Schools have their own individuality, reflecting the different influences to which they are subject. To a considerable degree they have to chart their own course and this chapter does not, therefore, presume to be a comprehensive guide to citizenship education which all should follow. It provides a summary of some of the paths and signposts to which conference participants attached value.

The aims of education for citizenship identified by NCC were described in the introductory chapter. The role of the individual within the community is inherent in these aims. Citizenship education, therefore, needs to be developed in active and experiential ways in real contexts. In this way pupils can acquire and practise life skills and supplement more formal ways of learning. This involves pupils going out into the community and the community coming into the school, a partnership between school and community in which each serves as a resource for the other.

In his address to the conference, Michael Duffy emphasised three elements necessary for citizenship which had been identified by Boateng (1989) in a paper to the commission: a sense of belonging; the capacity to gain access; the ability to participate. Without any one of these there is no citizenship. They are closely related and interdependent. While all are part of a vision of citizenship, the first is particularly concerned with a shared set of values. The second and third are related to attitudes, skills, knowledge and understanding which make that condition possible.

The School as a Community

The school itself is a community which consists not just of pupils and teachers but of all people who work in or have an interest in the school, including lunch time supervisors, ancillary or teaching support staff, cleaning staff, site supervisors, volunteers, parents and governors. Simply by being part of this community, members can acquire knowledge, understanding and skills, and have the opportunity to develop values and attitudes which contribute to citizenship education. The exercise of rights, responsibilities and duties is demonstrated and practised within the school. The school, therefore, is a principal resource for learning.

If the school is a model, what do people learn from the model? Is this the learning we seek to encourage? If not, what alterations should be made to the model? Citizenship education is thus intimately tied to the nature of the school. Equally, the future development of the school and its ethos cannot be separated from the development of citizenship education.

What is the school's vision? What is its purpose? Are its aims clear, understood and subscribed to by all? Is there clarity about values which underpin the aims? Do members of the school share in discussion of these values? Do they measure their own practice against the values? Are the values understood and shared by the wider community which the school serves? Given that we see our state as democratic, how democratic are our schools and in what ways can we make them more democratic?

If we are to be consistent we should aim to establish an ethos which reflects the vision and contributes to its attainment. The role of the head in shaping the ethos of the school is paramount: through the quality of leadership, style of management and organisational structures established; through appointments made; and through the quality of relationships fostered. Leadership enables and relies on: exploration of values; empowerment of people; collaboration; development planning; the setting of attainable targets; good communication to facilitate understanding of present reality and future goals; co-operation and partnership with the wider community; positive attitudes and behaviour.

It involves giving a clear sense of direction and modelling the attitudes and behaviour expected of others. This is very important where it is necessary to raise the awareness of staff and to develop the school by bringing about a change of ethos. As change progresses so the style of leadership may move from one of consultation to involving increasing levels of participation by staff and other groups connected with the school.

Are the values of the school made clear to applicants for appointment? Is support for these values probed during appointment procedures? Are governors involved in this process fully aware of the importance of this aspect? Do staff have clear job descriptions which embody the school's vision as exemplified in the written aims and objectives? Do they have appropriate delegated responsibility and the opportunity for initiative within the development plan structure? Do school policies embody the vision so that all staff have a clear sense of direction?

Personal Qualities and Relationships

The following qualities were suggested by conference members as important to citizenship education and capable of development through the ethos of the school: independence of thought; being well organised; self-esteem; sensitivity; empathy; respect for others; confidence; a sense of responsibility; ability in critical self-appraisal.

Such qualities are supported by a range of knowledge and skills. The development of such qualities, and of citizenship education in general, requires whole school involvement; it is the responsibility of all and the policies and practices related to it need to be owned by the whole school. It is a function of management to develop and encourage this by enabling people to share in the process of development.

Particular importance attaches to the quality of relationships and through this to self esteem. Self-esteem will affect the way an individual can relate to others, to the school and to the wider community. It will help to determine levels of confidence, personal happiness, the ability to succeed and quality of life. Self-esteem is, therefore, at the root of an ethos which fosters citizenship. In particular, low self-esteem produces inequality of opportunity. Self-esteem is therefore fundamental to an effective equal opportunities policy, an essential feature of a democratic education and is inherent in achieving a sense of belonging – one of the criteria for citizenship referred to above.

How is Self-Esteem Developed?

The process must start with the staff – all staff, not only teachers. If staff feel good, the pupils are more likely to. If staff are unhappy, disenchanted, cynical, this must influence the children in their care.

Management practices are crucial to staff self esteem and the following practices were identified as important:

> facilitating participation in the management and development of the school, aiming for a corporate or collegial organisation rather than one which is strongly hierarchical; giving people responsibility; praise and recognition; being interested; smiling; management by walking about (but not prowling); supporting, working alongside staff, being actively involved and thereby establishing trust; appraisal to improve performance and job satisfaction; criticism given in a constructive way which staff can handle, never giving on-the-spot admonishment; planning so staff can have success, reviewing constantly; always finding something good to say on a classroom visit; encouraging initiative.

For pupils, the same principles need to be applied, aiming, for example, to:

> build confidence; overcome suspicion; give responsibility; listen to what they say, and to their silences; provide time for reflection and for sharing thoughts with each other; use merits and get rid of demerits; involve them in their learning, in planning, organisation and evaluation; value all achievement; talk to children in an adult way; be polite; develop well balanced young people; satisfy a yearning for significance; develop a climate of openness.

Openness implies a willingness to share. This may be on a personal level or between ethnic or other cultural groups within the school. Children and staff can celebrate each other's festivals and share sorrow together. Black and white children may be paired deliberately and children from different ethnic groups helped to realise that all are in a continuous learning situation. In this climate children and staff can understand and be open with each other about the fact that people may make mistakes in an ethnic context through lack of knowledge. However, such an environment and approach is not risk free.

The school community needs to be characterised by respect for the individual and the needs of its members, by a sense of fairness and justice – in other words, helping to establish an understanding of the relationship between rights and responsibilities. Involving pupils in agreeing codes of behaviour, or a classroom contract, facilitates this understanding by relating it directly to pupil needs. Policies relating to pupils who for various reasons do not accept such codes need to be carefully worked out so that they derive from and are consistent with the ethos of the school.

The Whole Staff

School communities contain people other than teachers and pupils. What has been said about understanding and sharing values and about self-esteem applies to all who work in the school. This includes the right to, and indeed necessity of, involvement in training and the provision of support. Office staff are usually the first point of contact between school and visitors. The impression they give of the school and their commitment to it is, therefore, particularly important.

Lunchtime supervisors do not have the continuity and same range of contact with pupils which enables teachers to build strong relationships. Their designation as supervisors may be seen as indicative of an emphasis on control and almost suggests the likelihood of confrontation. How closely does the way they relate to pupils match teacher/pupil relationships? What strains are created if they do not? How can on-the-job training and support be given to untrained and maybe inexperienced people in this role? What steps can be taken to try to ensure that they enjoy parity of esteem? How can the school express its appreciation of their role? Are they invited to participate in school and staff functions?

Similar questions may be posed in relation to other groups working in school, including volunteers. Without consideration of such issues the inconsistencies which are likely to occur will create tensions which may undermine the intended ethos. What, for example, is the impact on afternoon school if pupils are in the lunchtime care of those who treat children differently from the norms which apply during the rest of the day?

Giving Pupils Responsibility Through Participation

Section 1 of the Education Reform Act talks of preparing pupils for the opportunities and experiences of adult life, which many would identify as an essential part of citizenship education. *Curriculum Guidance 8* refers to rights and responsibilities in several contexts. What, then, are the opportunities for responsibility which will help pupils to realise their citizenship? Do we approach them as pupils or students? How can we involve them in taking more responsibility for their own learning? By widening the range of responsibility we increase the opportunities to fulfil potential and move further from the measurement of success in purely academic terms.

The process of learning itself offers considerable scope for pupils to exercise responsibility. Group work in which students work collaboratively with a common purpose can be seen as the hub of citizenship. By varying group size and composition students learn to work with different people. Peer group tutoring in which students help each other to learn offers similar opportunities.

Students can be consulted about issues and topics which concern them, including the nature and process of their own learning. This can involve planning, agreeing targets, reviewing performance, contributing to reports, evaluating lessons and courses. Students can engage in negotiation about courses (e.g. pathways through option schemes or modular courses). They may also share in discussions at parents' evenings. Many schools have involved students in drawing up guidelines or policies on aspects of school life such as equality of opportunity, multi-cultural education, health education, behaviour, bullying and creating an effective learning environment.

Students can engage in the planning of school visits, work experience and community involvement. They can organise assemblies, run clubs, plan charity support and environmental projects. Schemes such as Young Enterprise and the Duke of Edinburgh Award are specifically organised to enable young people to undertake responsibility. Student councils not only provide responsibility but also give direct experience of a democratic process. This, however, makes it all the more important for the council to achieve something so that it is not discredited in the eyes of other students.

Some Issues Relating to Pupils' Responsibility

If we see the development of a young person in terms of progression

towards personal autonomy, we need learning experiences which will provide for the progressive development of skills and opportunities for
responsibility. There is a need to plan across phases. In particular, there is
the possibility of regression in expectation about the capacity for responsibility on transfer from primary to secondary phase. This emphasises the
value of cross-phase liaison in which primary and secondary teachers work
together, visit each others' schools, possibly exchange classes and organise
cross-phase projects, started in one school and completed in another.

How far can one go in developing personal autonomy in school? What is
the framework within which pupils exercise responsibility? Given that
pupils pass from infancy to adulthood within the years of formal education,
parents, students and schools are bound in a complex developing relationship. How do we prepare for, avoid or reconcile the potential conflicts
which may occur?

The Teacher's Role: Developing the Ability to Participate

It is important that teachers understand that their purpose is:

> to develop young people, to help them grow as individuals; to find better ways of
> helping them to learn; to develop skills which will help them to learn independently
> and 'prepare them for the opportunities, responsibilities and experiences of adult
> life' as required by the Education Reform Act.

Successful schools put children first. Teachers need to look at education
from the point of view of the learner. What do children experience? We
should ask ourselves what we remember of our own schooling as part of
reflection on what is significant in the learning process. A holistic view of
education is important rather than a narrow focus on a subject specialism.
Children should experience a wide variety of teaching and learning styles
as a matter of school policy.

It is important not to study citizenship simply as a theoretical subject
resembling some civics courses of the past. Theory and practice need to be
linked in active and experiential learning which provides contexts for the
acquisition of skills, knowledge and understanding. It is essential for students to have knowledge of how society works and evolves so that they can
exercise their skills more effectively. The list of useful skills is long but
will include those involved in:

> self-assessment; forming relationships; working with others; organisation; personal
> financial management; communication; gathering evidence; analysing evidence;
> decision making; expressing opinion in appropriate ways; debate; resolution of
> conflict.

Confronting issues of a controversial nature is inherent in citizenship
education, and itself requires a variety of skills. This process should lead to
the formulation of opinions and beliefs and is an essential element in moral
education.

Skills can be extended not only by the range of learning experiences provided by the teacher but by the involvement of adults other than teachers – ancillary staff, parent helpers, college students, employers and others from industry, police, the arts, the older generation, in fact, all sections of the wider community. By the same process young people increase their knowledge and understanding of the outside world.

The Key Role of the Tutor or Class Teacher

Citizenship education should infuse the whole curriculum and a carefully structured tutor system can help to ensure this. In a secondary school the tutor is the one person who should have oversight of the student's achievements in all spheres. The relationship between tutor and student and tutor and parents is therefore very important.

The tutor can help the pupil to understand the concept of educational entitlement and is likely to be the principal adult working with the pupil on Records of Achievement. In many secondary schools the tutor's role is growing significantly. Consideration needs to be given to this in initial teacher training, recruitment, induction and the provision of support systems.

The School and its Governors

The school, parents and governing body need to be in partnership. The governor's role includes support, monitoring, reflecting community expectations, asking questions and providing an additional and valuable means of communication between the school and the community it serves. By virtue of being governors, they can be seen as role models for active citizenship. The governing body also presents schools with a model of political processes and responsibilities.

Attachment to curricular areas is one way of enabling insight with a purpose. Schools might ask governors to be responsible for monitoring a theme within the curriculum. The cross-curricular themes, as preparation for adult life, may actually be the most accessible aspect of the curriculum for governors. The Speaker's Commisssion recommended that governing bodies should ask schools to develop strategies for developing and monitoring citizenship studies across the curriculum and should consider progress reports regularly.

Do the governors understand, share and support the school's ethos and the values on which it is based? Is this easier for some kinds of schools (e.g. aided schools) than others? Are there opportunities for governors and staff to share training?

There are issues concerning whether governing bodies are truly representative of the community. Are certain socio-economic or ethnic groups effectively disenfranchised? There is a need to demystify the role of governor and to make it more accessible by making deliberations more widely known, and by making documents more readable and readily available to the general public. Co-option of non-voting members on sub-committees is one way of widening representation and giving experience to people who may one day seek full membership. It is important that pupils, teachers and the wider community understand the role of governors as one aspect of the democratic process and, because of this, it is an area where there should be equality of opportunity.

Involving Parents and Others from the Community

The involvement in a school of members of the local community is a source of strength and of enrichment. It enhances the status of the teacher rather than threatens it. The presence of other adults, as helpers or as learners provides a strong message to pupils about the value attached to education. Education is a life-long process and older people have much to contribute.

There is a need to make school welcoming to parents who may feel reticent about venturing into a large, unfamiliar building. A reception desk staffed by pupils is one way of ensuring visitors are properly received and provides a valuable experience for the pupils involved. Extra efforts may be needed to engage some communities with no tradition of involvement. How well do teachers understand the community served by their school? How aware are they of the variety of communities within the general community and of their attitudes, values and beliefs? What are the views of the police, social workers and other groups? Community profiles indicating what it is like to live in an area can serve a useful purpose.

An audit of all community contacts and the use of adults other than teachers is a relatively simple and potentially rewarding task in raising awareness of their value and variety and opening eyes to further possibilities. The benefits of such involvement do not all flow one way. The school should see itself as a resource for the community and be fully aware of the ways in which it can contribute to the community while providing an enriched education for its students.

Summary

Citizenship education is inseparable from the ethos, climate or culture of the school. Ethos is a feeling of what the school is. It is shaped by all that happens in the school – the style of management, the relationships which exist between all participants in the school community, the interaction with the wider community, the nature of the curriculum, the way it is organised and assessed, the way students learn, the environment in which they learn.

Michael Duffy, in his concluding remarks to the conference, summed up the nature of citizenship education:

Citizenship is central to all that we learn in school but it is not so much a matter of 'to learn' as 'to be'. Therefore, teachers and others must practise what they teach. No matter what experiences you put into the curriculum, if the culture is wrong, you will not create citizens.

References

Boateng, P. (1989) Unpublished paper to the Commission on Citizenship Seminar, 14–15th April, 1989.

Speaker's Commission on Citizenship (1990) *Encouraging Citizenship*. London: HMSO.

CHAPTER 3

Cross-Curricularity

Sue Harrison and George Knights

The purpose of this chapter is to contribute to the thinking of management teams in schools as they examine the place of citizenship in the curriculum. It explores the concept of cross-curricularity, first, within the context of a model of curriculum planning common in schools and then within an alternative model. It then applies this to the theme of citizenship. Accepted strategies for auditing the curriculum are considered alongside a particular notion of mapping. The latter involves teachers in processes which mirror those consistent with education for citizenship.

The chapter recognises that education is a life-long activity and it is written with all learners in mind. Therefore, although it refers throughout to students and schools, readers will be able to relate these terms to the age group and institution relevant to them.

In addition to implementing the ten subjects which form the core and foundation of the National Curriculum, schools are expected to incorporate a range of cross-curricular elements. *Curriculum Guidance 3: The Whole Curriculum* describes these elements as the 'ingredients which tie together the broad education of the individual and augment what comes from the basic curriculum'.

Out of this context there has emerged a conception of the whole curriculum consisting primarily of the core and foundation subjects and the cross-curricular elements. A whole curriculum defined in this way can be challenged on several counts. First, it reflects a view of curriculum as content rather than process. Second, if the curriculum is seen as whole then it is necessarily bounded. Establishing boundaries imposes limits, inevitably arbitrary, as to what is possible or appropriate for students. This could deny students access to a range of experiences which may arise naturally in the process of learning. And third, a fragmented and compartmentalised curriculum militates against learners trying to make interconnections across a range of experiences.

A content model of curriculum, described in terms of subjects, is that upon which the work in most British schools has been based for many years. Even in primary schools where attempts have been made to develop a more holistic view of the curriculum there has been pressure for the frame of reference to be subject based. The emergence of the National Curriculum has reinforced this and political rhetoric has been targeted at making this model of the curriculum more dominant. Consequently, a content view of the curriculum, although extensively criticised in the past, is becoming increasingly less open to challenge. There is a decrease in the willingness either to engage in a fundamental appraisal of this model, at a time when it is being reinforced by legislation, or to invest in exploring alternative models.

It is important to acknowledge that the concept of cross-curricularity, including the elements it embodies in terms of skills, dimensions and themes, has arisen out of a particular view of curriculum which itself is a manifestation of a specific political ideology. For Carr (1991) the National Curriculum is 'the centrepiece of a general set of "Educational Reforms" designed to create a free-market system of education and to transform the curriculum into goods and services to be "delivered" to parents and pupils by teachers and schools'. Any consideration of the cross-curricular elements should not ignore the context in which they have arisen. This is especially the case in relation to the theme of citizenship which by its very nature embodies political and moral issues. It is important, therefore, to explore alternative views of the curriculum – and by implication cross-curricularity – in order to discover whether they may provide a more effective means of developing citizenship.

An alternative, holistic view examines the idea of curriculum in terms of the experiences of learners. If these experiences are considered to comprise discrete entities then this holistic view implies that learning is more than the sum of the parts.

Research over many years suggests that students learn from a variety of experiences from which they seek to make interconnections. It is the making of these links which strengthens understanding and provides a framework for further learning. In attempts to support curriculum planning and monitoring, learning, invariably, has been differentiated into discrete types; most commonly knowledge and understanding, skills and attitudes. Whilst this differentiation may have some merit for planning and monitoring, it constitutes a fundamental misrepresentation of the nature of the learning process. As Reid (1986) points out, 'knowledge and understanding are distinguishable conceptually, though inseparable existentially'. A holistic view recognises that it is not possible to separate knowledge from skills or understanding within the learning process.

A curriculum defined in terms of learning experiences focuses on the process, as opposed to the content, of learning. It suggests that the curriculum is a dynamic, interactive and, above all, contextualised process. From this perspective, it could be argued that cross-curricularity is a meaningless concept, being external to the student and hence not concomitant with their internalised experiences. Alternatively, cross-curricularity could be redefined in terms of the processes that enable students to establish coherence and continuity across a range of educational experiences.

School Values

Recent initiatives concerning the processes of development planning in schools have emphasised as the first step the establishment, or review, of statements of values and principles. A school's value statement will need to articulate views, in particular, on student learning and the role of the teacher.

Student Ownership of Learning

It is fundamental to the concept of a process curriculum that learning is interactive and collaborative. Such learning is most effective when students have an understanding and sense of ownership of the processes they are involved in. Ownership may be thought of in terms of the learner being able:

– to relate the current experience to prior learning;
– to recognise and accept the purpose for the learning;
– to develop a unique learning pathway, based on making personal decisions and taking responsibility for them.

Given these three conditions it is hoped that students would be able to approach their learning with confidence by building on expectations of worthwhileness, enjoyment and intrinsic reward. In turn, this would empower them to take greater responsiblity for future learning.

The Role of the Teacher

Creating an environment which promotes a sense of ownership of the learning process will require a fundamental reorientation in the role of the teacher. A conception of teaching and learning predicated on the belief that the teacher is, essentially, responsible for leading the student to and through predetermined learning pathways needs to be challenged. An alternative, consistent with students owning the learning process, is that the teacher should be a facilitator or enabler, responding to the perceived needs of the students in the light of their prior learning. This recognises that the teacher and the students together have responsibility for evaluating previous, present and future learning. Such collaboration helps to avoid any possible mismatch between what the teacher does and what the students need to do. This approach recognises that teaching is not about giving knowledge but about enabling students to understand how to engage with knowledge; that is, to come into a state of knowing. From this students acquire the ability to analyse, criticise, apply, change, challenge and so on.

Citizenship

Citizenship is a complex and contested concept which historically has its roots in ethics and politics. It is not the aim of this chapter to examine the concept in depth but to question how it is, or how it may be, conceived within the curriculum. Whatever else, it is our view that citizenship is concerned with developing the skills and understanding relating to:

(1) decision-making;
(2) establishing and developing interpersonal relationships;
(3) exercising rights and responsibilities;
(4) participating in and contributing to the community.

It follows, therefore, that education for citizenship should be planned in terms of process, for many aspects of citizenship are developed most appropriately in the context of active and interactive modes of learning.

The development of a process curriculum acknowledges that the school is a social institution, its life being built on the interactions of the people who make up that learning community. Fundamental to education for citizenship is the active participation of all who work in schools – students, teachers, parents, governors and others – in all aspects of the school's life. Within the school there is, therefore, a need to nurture an ethos wherein key issues and values can be openly and fully discussed for 'Schools need to practise what they seek to promote', (Schools Council 1981).

Establishing a forum for debate and discussion about citizenship would provide opportunities for staff to come together to explore meanings about their practice and to clarify the principles upon which the work of the school is based. As dialogue develops teachers would be challenged to clarify and articulate their understandings of the breadth and scope of what is being provided for students. In turn, this would require re-definition against a broader background of awareness and understanding of others.

One of the reasons why schools do not readily adopt a holistic approach to the curriculum stems from the difficulty of establishing effective dialogue between staff working in discrete subject areas. Recent research (Hargreaves, 1991) lends credence to Lortie's argument that the individualistic, present-orientated and conservative occupational culture of teachers, together with the cellular patterns of organisation within which they practise, militates against long-term, collaborative planning (Lortie, 1975). Indeed it has been claimed that even when given the opportunity to engage collaboratively with colleagues, many teachers show a reluctance to do so (Blenkin, Edwards & Kelly, 1992). Nevertheless, if teachers can be supported in understanding that they have a great deal to offer from their existing practice, then the positive effects of working together can be considerable.

Auditing the Curriculum

In order to move forwards schools need to have clarity about what is happening already and what they hope to achieve. Currrent practice is reviewed in a variety of ways and one commonly used process is known as an audit. The purpose of a curriculum audit is to find out what is happening in the school. Several recently produced documents advocate that an audit should be undertaken as a prerequisite for entering into a programme of development planning. *Curriculum Guidance 3* identifies the audit as step 1 in whole curriculum planning, while Hargreaves et al (1989) suggest that the purposes of an audit are:

- to clarify the state of the school and to identify strengths on which to build and weaknesses to be rectified;
- to provide a basis for selecting priorities for development.

An audit thus serves to provide a description of existing work as a basis for future planning activity. Undertaking an audit commonly involves seeking information from teachers about curriculum areas for which they are responsible. Teachers indicate where their work in the classroom meets specific and predetermined criteria. This information is then collated. The criteria may be based on programmes of study from National Curriculum subjects, or on aspects of the cross-curricular themes taken from *Curriculum Guidance 4* to *8*.

Three inherent weaknesses emerge from this process. First, an audit is seen as a linear process. This, inevitably, inhibits the process from going back and forth. Second, it is an inventory which analyses curriculum provision in terms of a series of component parts separate from its overall context. Third, the establishment of pre-determined criteria makes a priori assumptions about what should comprise the curriculum and therefore, by implication, indicates what is missing. We have argued above for a model of curriculum based on the experiences of students, rather than on pre-determined content. Further, we have implied that learning is about change. Therefore an audit, which endeavours to record and to make explicit the status quo, is inconsistent with this curriculum model.

It is all too easy for schools to embark on a task which may generate a feeling of having done something valuable but which may be of limited practical use. The undertaking of an audit needs to recognise the nature and the limitations of the process. What is missing from the process is an exploration, amongst colleagues, of meanings and understandings regarding the nature of the experiences being provided for students. This is particularly relevant in relation to the provision of the cross-curricular skills, themes and dimensions. The challenge for schools is to provide experiences which are coherent and which ensure progression for students. Dialogue which supports staff in coming to a shared understanding of this challenge will assist the process.

From Audit to Map: Developing Dialogue

A process model of curriculum has, as a central plank, the notion of inter-action – between student and teacher, between student and student and, most importantly, between student and the learning environment. The process model is underpinned by the view that the development of learning is based upon questioning, challenging and debating difference. It fosters the expression and exploration of different ideas and provides the means of promoting better understanding and greater clarity of fundamental issues. If this is true for students then it should be reflected in the professional work undertaken by teachers when they endeavour to prepare learning environments which embody these values.

This implies that school managers should identify time for teachers to work together. Collaboration can be extended to include other stakeholders such as parents and governors, thus creating a model of citizenship education which embraces a community context. The challenge for schools is to establish strategies which enable dialogue and debate about the deeper meanings of education and which lead to continuous improvement in the learning of students, teachers and, indeed, all members of the community. One such strategy could be the process of curriculum mapping.

Curriculum Mapping

An audit is, essentially, descriptive. A map, on the other hand, can be inter-pretative. Maps enable multiple interpretations, or readings. Thus a process of mapping may provide a more realistic, and useful, view of the curriculum as well as a means for its exploration.

It was suggested above that teachers need to work together to explore understandings and meanings about the work which they undertake with students. The importance of teacher involvement in the process of curriculum development is acknowledged in *Curriculum Guidance 3* in that 'their involvement ensures that the full range of views is heard and that conflict-ing opinions are debated'. This debate needs to proceed until all are aware of, and can appreciate, what others understand about their work in a partic-ular context. The acknowledgement of multiple realities cautions against any simplistic establishment of consensus.

In order to appreciate the power of focusing the curriculum in this way it is helpful to consider the metaphor of a map.

(a) A whole map does not exist, in the same way that there is no whole curriculum. Nevertheless, a map provides a broad picture and clarity about the relationships between the constituent parts. A map provides a means of understanding these inter-relationships and of supporting effective engagements with what it represents. It enables consideration to flow from the particular to the general and back again, thus estab-lishing that component parts can only be understood in their wider context. Dialogues which seek to develop shared meanings are analogous to seeking these understandings.

(b) A map is an attempt to portray a certain temporal reality; the situation at a point in time. However, the inter-relationships between the phenomena represented are dynamic and change is inevitable over time. To this extent maps are contingent. What they portray may or may not be deducible from the map itself. Maps not only show the 'what' but also give indications about the 'why'. Thus, in order to gain detailed insights into what a map is showing it is important to seek additional information from elsewhere. The curriculum is similarly contingent and mapping puts current practice into its wider socio-historical and political contexts.

(c) Maps are modified over time, partly as a result of improved cartographical techniques and partly as a result of changes in the phenomena represented. Similarly modifications are made in curriculum maps. Some stem from research that provides a better understanding about the nature of knowledge and learning. Others emerge from the development of deeper meanings about educational values as a result of conflict or negotiation.

(d) Maps can have different scales. At times it is important to focus on one particular part of the map. At this point a different scale can be applied. By so doing, the amount of detailed information available increases significantly without any loss of overall perspective or sense of inter-relatedness. Direct application of this principle to the curriculum makes for easy interchange between, say, broad notions of citizenship in the curriculum and a detailed exploration of specific statements.

(e) Maps are two-dimensional representations of more complex realities. However, it is possible to represent height by the use of contours. In terms of curriculum mapping, the two dimensional reality might consist of learning experiences within a particular curriculum area. The third dimension could then be an exploration of some element of learning not specific to that area but permeating all learning, for example, promoting equal opportunities.

A mapping process needs to focus on the curriculum in terms of student experiences but in relation to wider value questions. Elsewhere in this book teachers are invited to explore citizenship from the perspective of their own subject areas. This will not be enough. Teachers with various specialisms need to come together so that through dialogue and collaborative planning they can put their work into a wider curriculum context.

In relation to citizenship, *Curriculum Guidance 8* identifies a large number of areas for potential study, for example:

• a study of history and culture from different perspectives;

- family life-cycles, patterns of marriage and family structure and how these change;
- legal responsibilities and rights.

None of these fits neatly into a single subject area. Indeed, several subject areas might support each of these statements. It is this overlap which provides a starting point for dialogue. The strategy below assumes the bringing together of teachers who believe that through their work they can contribute to a particular statement for a given group of students.

General statements, such as those above, need interpretation in context. Inviting teachers to identify where such statements might be realised within their work enables discussion about their meanings and debate can promote further clarification. Certain ideas may need to be returned to at later stages in the student's schooling but at increasingly higher levels of complexity. Awareness of this enables teachers to be more effective in helping students to make inter-connections, and by so doing contribute to coherence and progression in their learning.

Such an activity as this is, however, only a first step. Of itself it does not address what students will actually be doing. Consequently teachers need to consider: relevant aspects of their aims and values which will influence their planning for responding to each particular statement; classroom interactions and ways in which students are engaged in the learning process; what students will have learned from these experiences and how these outcomes are consistent with the school's values. In-service activities which assist with these processes can be found in publications such as Edwards and Pathan (1993) and Tilley and King (1991).

Summary

The metaphor of mapping suggests that teachers need to address aspects of the inter-relationships between the learning experiences being provided. It takes account of the conflict which will manifest itself in debate, question and challenge between colleagues.

Schools are recognised here to be learning communities. As such, they will need to support democratic forms of decision-making and to establish systems which are participatory and collegiate. This is in keeping with a professional model of accountability. What is being advocated here is a departure from the more orthodox view of the school curriculum. Teachers are being invited to participate in the development of a culture which promotes critical debate about the curriculum. This approach recognises that developing the curriculum requires questioning and challenging, then in turn debating, making decisions and acting upon them. Developing the curriculum in this way thus entails processes, skills and attitudes which are at the heart of participative citizenship.

24

References

Blenkin, G.M., Edwards, G. and Kelly, A.V. (1992) *Change and The Curriculum* . London: Paul Chapman Publishing Ltd.

Carr, W. (1991) 'Education for Citizenship' *British Journal of Educational Studies*, Vol.XXXIX, No. 4, pp.373–385.

Edwards, J. and Pathan, L. (eds) (1993) *Cross-curricular INSET and Resources Pack*. Cambridge: Pearson.

Hargreaves, A. (1991) 'Contrived Collegiality: Micropolitics of Teacher Collaboration' in Blase, J. (ed) *The Politics of Life in Schools* . London: Sage Publications.

Hargreaves D. *et al* (1989) *Planning for School Development: Advice to Governors, Headteachers and Teachers*. London: DES.

Lortie, D.C. (1975) *School Teacher: A Sociological Study*. Chicago: University of Chicago Press.

Reid, L. A. (1986) *Ways of Understanding and Education*. London: Heinemann Educational.

Schools Council (1981) *The Practical Curriculum*. London: Schools Council.

Tilley, G. and King, D. (eds) (1991) *Cross-Curricular Issues: an INSET Manual for Secondary Schools*. London: Longman.

CHAPTER 4

Citizenship and the other Cross-Curricular Themes

ECONOMIC AND INDUSTRIAL UNDERSTANDING

Janice Felce

'Economic and Industrial Understanding (EIU) is important for people of all ages and in all parts of the world. In the case of young people it must be seen as an essential component within their preparation for the responsibilities and challenges which are part of an ever more complex world. To gain awareness of the economic forces which shape our world is to gain more power and control over our own lives. It helps us understand the link between our own economic decisions and those of others. This understanding will enable us all to contribute more fully as producers, consumers and citizens to the idea of a fair and prosperous society.'

(Tilley and King 1991)

EIU and its Links with Citizenship

The above rationale for including EIU in the curriculum, produced by a group of teachers in Leicestershire, highlights the importance of EIU and its close link with the qualities of citizenship. Many of the forces at work in society today are economic in nature and only through understanding these forces, their origins and operation, can young people contribute fully to society in their roles as citizens.

Central to EIU is the idea that resources are scarce so that choices have to be made between alternatives. This has implications for all – individuals, regions, nations and the world. Young people may be seen as present and future citizens operating at several levels, who already have rights, responsibilities and duties and these will increase as they reach adulthood. By helping pupils to acquire and understand essential information and by providing them with opportunities and incentives in all aspects of school life EIU contributes to their preparation for citizenship.

EIU in the Curriculum

Economic and industrial understanding is an essential part of every pupil's curriculum. It helps them understand the world in which they live and prepares them for life and work in an industrialised society. Young people should be well informed about the world in which they live; the human, political, economic, social and environmental factors that influence and shape it, how and why it came to be as it is. Throughout their lives they will have to face and make economic decisions. They will need to make choices about how they participate in and contribute to the economy through their work. They will have decisions to make about finance and which goods and services to spend money on. They will form views on public issues, many controversial, such as the environmental effects of economic development, which will require economic understanding to consider and debate the arguments put forward.

Consideration of controversial issues is a necessary and important part of EIU and contributes to the development of citizenship in that it helps young people to form and act upon ideas and opinions shaped by their own values. There are opportunities for wide consideration of different economic, political and moral views. Contexts and activities for developing EIU in the curriculum equip young people with relevant knowledge, understanding, skills and attitudes which, as well as contributing to personal and social development, empower young people to participate in society. Analysis of NCC guidance reveals that there is considerable overlap between EIU and citizenship in the knowledge content specified. Certainly many of the skills and attitudes identified in the EIU document are requisites for any programme devised to develop qualities of citizenship in young people.

Planning, Managing and Co-ordinating EIU in Schools

EIU can be acquired without learning elaborate theories which have tended to characterise the teaching of Economics in the past. It is concerned with pupils understanding key words or concepts which help formulate our experience and the way we think about economic issues as well as the skills to investigate, question, analyse and critically review information, views and opinions. Several key ideas can be approached in simple ways in the early primary years and treatment of them can become more refined as children grow older. Practical activities and relevance to their everyday life should be major features of this development. Links with industry and the wider community and various forms of enterprise activities can make enjoyable and stimulating contributions. Both primary and secondary schools, when planning provision for economic and industrial understanding, will find that the existing curriculum provides opportunities and foundations for developing the work further.

Table 4.1

EXAMPLES OF CLASSROOM ACTIVITIES ILLUSTRATING HOW EIU AND CITIZENSHIP CAN BE DEVELOPED IN FOUNDATION SUBJECTS

FOUNDATION SUBJECT	EIU	CITIZENSHIP
ENGLISH Reading literature e.g. *Animal Farm*	Organisation of work Specialist roles Interdependence Styles of management Command economics	Discussion of freedom and lack of freedom Rules and laws Co-operation and conflict Human rights
MATHEMATICS Weighing, measuring and costing materials offered for sale in a school tuck shop project	Costs Buying and selling Work and employment Health and safety	Honesty Responsibility Trust Fairness
SCIENCE Design and test new materials for a playground	Needs Costs and benefits Health and safety	Public services Community service Local government Legislation
TECHNOLOGY As a team design a tie for a prominent person to promote Oxfam	Advertising Scarce resources Choices Manufacturing	Co-operation Interdependence Pressure groups Public life
HISTORY Study the influence of the Rochdale Pioneers in the development of co-operative societies	Wholesaling Retailing Profit Distribution of wealth Employment	Social structures Community and co-operation Work Welfare Responsibility to others
GEOGRAPHY Re-locate a community faced with extinction from an active volcano	Needs and wants Choices Resources Interdependence	Systems and structures Rules and laws Society Responsibility
MODERN LANGUAGE A work based project undertaken in a company in Europe	Organisation of industry How a firm operates Interdependence Employment in the EEC	Rules and regulations Different societies and culture Decision making International co-operation Rights and responsibilities of a European Community Citizen
MUSIC Write a letter to a local supermarket complaining about the selection for the background music. Suggest a new 2 hour programme.	Needs and wants Buying and selling Patterns of shopping Advertising Customer satisfaction	Consumer rights Standards Values Life style

Table 4.2 CROSS-CURRICULAR PROJECTS

A PRIMARY: JEWEL IN THE CROWN

CONTEXT: St Gregory's RC Lower School, Northampton
Key Stage 1 cross-curricular topic on rocks

OUTLINE
A visit to a local quarry stimulated children's interest in rocks and precious stones. The teacher encouraged this interest by introducing the topic of Jewels and their importance in ceremonies and rituals. One outcome was the re-enactment by the children of the State Opening of Parliament using their own designed and made artefacts which supported the development of understanding of the role of Parliament in Democracy.

CURRICULUM LINKS:	Humanities, English, Maths, Technology, Science, Citizenship, EIU, Careers
COMMUNITY LINKS:	Industry
	Dignitaries: Town Mayor, MP etc.
	Jeweller

KEY CONCEPTS

EIU:	Needs, Scarcity Value, Resources, Production
CITIZENSHIP:	Rules, Laws, Responsibilities, Public Service, Democracy in Action

---

B SECONDARY: BERLIN WALL

CONTEXT: Boothville Middle School, Northampton
Key Stage 3 Collaborative Project on 'European Awareness' undertaken in Humanities, Technology and Modern Languages.

OUTLINE
This project focused on the concept of 'FREEDOM'. The rise and fall of the Berlin Wall became the central theme in a project on Germany. Pupils used cardboard boxes to build a wall to divide the school into East and West Boothlin using skills and techniques learned from representatives from local builders. Each pupil had identity cards and papers, guards patrolled the wall and freedom was restricted. The final outcome was the dramatic representation of a significant event in their lifetime – the fall of 'the wall' – to an outside audience.

CURRICULUM LINKS:	English, Maths, History, Geography, Technology, Music, Art, Citizenship, EIU
COMMUNITY LINKS:	Industry, local apprentices, VI form students

KEY CONCEPTS

EIU:	Standard of living, wealth distribution, economic growth, trade, different economics and societies
CITIZENSHIP:	Rights, responsibilities, freedom, democracy

EIU can be developed within most subjects (see Table 4.1). It is a two-way process: subjects provide opportunities to develop economic and industrial understanding and the economy provides contexts relevant to pupils' lives in which to develop subject knowledge, understanding and skills. Table 4.2 summarises two cross-curricular projects and indicates how they contributed to core and foundation subjects and components of citizenship and EIU. Careful planning will be required to ensure that provision across subjects is part of a coherent whole school policy, one of the main aims of which should be the development of awareness and understanding, in young people, of the inter-relationship between EIU and Citizenship.

References

Tilley, G. and King, D. (eds) (1991) *Cross-Curricular Issues: an INSET Manual for Secondary Schools.* London:Longmans.

HEALTH EDUCATION

Terry Brown and Janet Edwards

Health education and education for citizenship have consistently played a part in the formal and informal curriculum of British schools. Terminology has varied historically, reflecting prevailing medical, social and political priorities and consequent purpose, content and methodology.

NCC Guidance

The National Curriculum Council has issued advice to schools in *Curriculum Guidance 5, Health Education*, and *Curriculum Guidance 8, Education for Citizenship*. Each suggests appropriate areas of study, and an approach which applies to the individuals and the school both as a community itself and as part of the wider community.

In Health Education the 'knowledge, understanding, skills and attitudes which most pupils could be expected to have acquired by the end of each key stage' (p.11) are outlined in a framework of nine components, based upon current health concerns. These are: substance use and misuse, sex education, family life education, safety, health-related exercise, food and nutrition, personal hygiene, environmental aspects of health education, and psychological aspects of health education. It is suggested that the 'overlapping interests of individual, group and community health . . . permeate health education' and that 'at each key stage pupils should be offered experiences which allow them to develop understanding and skills in each of these three areas' (p.3).

Education for Citizenship suggests a framework for curriculum debate of eight 'essential components': community, a pluralist society, being a citizen, the family, democracy in action, the citizen and the law, work, employment and leisure, and public services. Unlike health education, these are not differentiated according to key stage. However, the document does recommend the progressive broadening of the focus of work and activities from the school community (key stage 1) through the local community (key stage 2) to national and international communities (key stages 3,4). Such a strategy would lead at key stage 1, for example, to closer attention to the family and community than to other components.

For Health Education 'Schools have a responsibility to provide pupils with accurate information about health matters, to help them clarify the attitudes and values which influence health choices and to promote the acquisition of healthy patterns of behaviour' (p.2), and 'much of the teaching...will be based on the active involvement of pupils' in order to encourage 'individual responsibility, awareness and informed decision-making' (p.7). Education for citizenship 'develops the knowledge, skills and attitudes necessary for exploring, making informed decisions about and exercising responsibilities and rights in a democratic society' (p.2).

The Health-Promoting School

Effective schools have the well-being of all their members as central to their purpose. They value the contributions of all partners in their communities. Partnerships with health professionals in their localities (in health centres, GP practices, facilities for the elderly, hospitals, playgroups etc) and with voluntary organisations (charities, religious groups, clubs etc) should ensure good collaborative relationships for everyone's benefit. The health educator has a role in ensuring that issues which are often seen as the preserve of the professional (doctor, social worker, nutritionist) are the responsibility of, and accessible to, each individual provided that the appropriate information is made available and understandable. With this assistance young people gain autonomy.

The well-managed school maintains high standards of cleanliness and decoration in its buildings, looks after the quality of the environment in its grounds, provides safe exercise facilities, pays attention to the balance of the catering offered and uses resources wisely. In these and other ways the institution promotes the message of health.

Health Education is an assembly of a wide range of topics which does not have the benefit of a long tradition of teaching in a specific discipline. Indeed it has often been thought of as a series of science-based topics with concerns of social or moral issues closely attached to them. From an organisational point of view these can result in modules such as Physical Fitness or Preparation for Family Life under the umbrella of Health Education. On the other hand health education has been considered as a broader, more value-laden part of the curriculum; one which is no longer considered as a single subject on the timetable, but may appear in PSE or tutorial programmes, or may be found across the curriculum in History, English, Home Economics or Biology. Extra-curricular activities (sports, camping, Duke of Edinburgh schemes etc) add greatly to students' experience. In many ways therefore the school may help to educate healthy young people – the future parents of the next generation. After the legal school-leaving age no institution has the opportunity of access to the whole cohort of people of one particular age. The school has a great opportunity to influence the long-term health of the community.

Healthy attitudes and good personal relationships are vital contributors to a healthy lifestyle. The health-promoting school creates a healthy physical and social environment which encourages self-confidence and self-esteem as well as promoting good physical health in all its members. Both themes have an underlying philosophy of empowering young people while encouraging and supporting their personal and social development. Through citizenship we aim to enable young people to appreciate that values, beliefs and moral codes change over time and are influenced by experience. There are parallels to be found in the 'health career' of a young person, when they are made aware of the external influences on personal decision-making and, ultimately, on choice over health-related issues such as smoking. In taking stock of their own position on a social and moral issue such as contraception or abortion, young people need time to compare values and beliefs held by themselves and others in order to find the common ground, and to consider the moral dilemmas, both personal and social. Informed decision-making needs to take account of the difficulty that the difference between right and wrong is not always straightforward. Respect for different ways of living, different beliefs and opinions, permeates much of the work done in health education on relationships – within families, between friends and in the community.

The Overlaps with Citizenship

Analysis of the subject matter contained in the components of health education and education for citizenship reveals that there is sufficient overlap to enable simultaneous attention. The table (4.3) sets out such an analysis and shows how, in particular, the community and family components of citizenship education overlap with health education.

Thus in knowledge content there is much overlap between health education and citizenship education, and in purpose too the themes have much in common – as in empowerment, personal development and preparation for adult life.

Conclusion

In many ways, therefore, the school may help to educate healthy young people – the future parents of the next generation. After the legal school-leaving age no institution has the opportunity of access to the whole cohort of people of one particular age. The school has great opportunity to influence the long-term health of the community.

Citizenship involves a person being in relationship with others in a locality. The healthy community needs to be aware of the varying requirements of its members. In the family and at school the opportunity exists to lay firm foundations for cooperative lifestyles ensuring that young people are ready to take their place in the community and to work collaboratively for their own good and the good of others. Citizenship education and health education are contributors with much in common.

Table 4.3

CITIZENSHIP

HEALTH	Community	A pluralist society	Being a citizen	The family	Democracy in action	The citizen and the law	Work employment and leisure	Public services
Substance use and misuse	4		2					
Sex education	2 3 4	3	3	2 3 4				
Family life education	1 2 4		2	1 2 3 4				
Safety			2					
Health related exercise							3	
Food and nutrition		4						
Personal hygiene								
Environmental aspects	2 4	2 4	2 4	2 4			2	3
Psychological aspects	1 2 4	1 2 4	1 2	1 2 3 4		2	2	

The table indicates where overlap occurs in relation to the components for each key stage.
The numbers in the cells indicate the key stage where overlap occurs e.g. the Safety component of Health Education overlaps with the Being a Citizen component of Citizenship Education in Key Stage 2

- help pupils to acquire and understand essential information on which to base the development of their skills, values, and attitudes towards citizenship.

The framework for citizenship education can be paraphrased as being about the concepts of rights, responsibilities and participation. Thus the link with the idea of the role-related curriculum is very clear. Citizenship can be expressed as being about enabling young people to explore their roles in relationship to the society in which they live, work, relax, form social bonds and operate as social beings. Careers education and guidance, as described by NCC, HMI and in the article by Law, covers conceptual development over precisely the same areas. From the point of view of the child it is unhelpful for the development of such concepts to separate the rights of citizens as laid down, or not laid down, in a constitutional document, from the rights of workers in law or in an employment contract. Similarly the strand **self**, as identified in the NCC CEG document, is described in terms of 'qualities, attitudes, values, abilities, strengths, limitations, potential and needs', while the NCC citizenship document gives a more detailed list of the attitudes, moral codes and values which contribute to promoting positive attitudes to society, and particularly to democratic society (for example, 'independence of thought on social and moral issues' and 'an enterprising and persistent approach to tasks and challenges'). Thus a school could take a conceptual approach to the role-related curriculum and build up, using contexts from CEG and citizenship, a coherent core programme of study.

In both areas of study however, there are distinctive components which are defined by NCC as part of the entitlement curriculum, although this term is not used. In CEG the components are more an issue of planned experiences and opportunities, whereas in citizenship the components are defined in terms of knowledge or 'contexts for citizenship' such as:

- work, employment and leisure;
- public services.

Both of these have clear links with a careers programme. Six other contexts, where the links are less explicit, are also listed.

NCC defines the components of a CEG programme as follows :

Careers Education: a planned programme in all four key stages;
Access to Information;
Experience of Work;
Access to Individual Guidance;
Recording Achievement and Planning for the future .

Managing the Curriculum

Thus schools have the task of designing a curriculum which incorporates all these elements around a central concept core, the core providing a focus for the work. In terms of management, there are many models for the successful implementation of the role-related curriculum. *Curriculum Guidance 3* suggested that such work could be planned within a PSE programme, within a separate timetable slot, wholly within Core and Foundation subjects or using other techniques such as long block timetabling.

At secondary level it would be possible to use the structure of a faculty of Personal and Social Education incorporating all aspects of student support including personal, vocational, academic and pastoral guidance. The faculty must have organisational parity with other faculties and thus have the 'clout' to influence the work of the other faculties to coordinate the experience of students into a coherent whole, perhaps through techniques such as mapping of the curriculum. Ungoed-Thomas, at a TACADE conference in April 1992, drew on observational experience to suggest that the keys to positive cross-curricular development included:

- direct involvement of the senior management team in fostering links;
- developing team working across curriculum areas;
- building from where the strengths of the school lie – be it in staff, community links, school setting or other.

As a starting point, some analysis of the teaching and learning styles used by teachers could be used to raise issues of value, understanding and purpose. Law (1992b) suggests the following as styles which contribute to the educating concept of careers education and guidance:

Paying attention to presentations;
Seeking information and impressions;
Forming explanations and hypotheses;
Advocating a point of view;
Responding to issues with personal opinions;
Practising skills and strategies;
Disclosing personally held material;
Acting out imagined situations;
Contacting adults in the community.

Such styles would seem to be common to all aspects of the role-related curriculum and a useful starting point for whole school curriculum development.

Next steps

One of the issues for schools is how to have a dynamic curriculum which can examine past understandings in the context of current and future developments. In careers terms the rate of change in the world of work continues to be high, and educating young people in careers must take account of this. The changes which are taking place are not only in the location and type of definition was found to reflect the feelings of the public by the findings of Fogelman's survey of secondary schools (Fogelman, 1991).

Much of the debate about citizenship education has moved to considering how to include the concept in the school curriculum and teach it effectively. This is probably not surprising in view of the pace of education reform in recent years, but to ignore the initial debates is to fail to recognise some of the suppositions being made. Marshall's definition of citizenship is the defining of a process not a goal. As schools strive to present their curricula in a balanced and constructive way, they have to recognise that there is indeed no consensus about either citizenship or environmental issues. Ideas range from a society adhering to a capitalist market exchange system (Barrie, 1989), to a society with an established welfare platform to enable participation (Dahrendorf, 1989). Thus I would suggest that the debate about what citizenship is has become bound up in ideas about the distribution of wealth and the efficiency of production systems.

Against this background, schools need to encourage all pupils to respond to the view that the environment is a common heritage, that there is a common duty to maintain, protect and improve its quality, to consider how societies can prudently and rationally utilise resources and how, as individuals, pupils can make informed responses to the need to protect the environment (NCC, 1990e). A crucial issue for schools and pupils will be to try and reconcile the need for food production, the provision of health care and shelter facilities with a growing awareness that the environment is more often than not placed at risk by the means of production employed to provide those facilities. Concepts of *rationality* (Merton, 1970) and *efficiency* may also need consideration by comparing the moral, spiritual and political dimensions of decision-making.

Fortunately schools, especially primary schools, have a long tradition of including study of the environment in their classrooms, 'nature tables' being one of its earliest manifestations. In 1980 David Bellamy (on BBC2's Horizon programme 'Sustainable Resources', 15th November), sharpened the focus of environmental concerns by proposing six 'pillars of conservation', which some schools adopted as the principles by which to guide their curriculum. These *pillars* may be summarised as:

- there is a need for a diverse genetic bank, especially to ensure continued food production;
- all life depends ultimately upon food production by plants, using the sun's energy;
- diverse habitats are little studied and may contain unknown sources of medicine;
- clean air and water are finite resources;
- energy sources are finite;
- humans seem to need wild places for their spiritual and physical well-being.

It is interesting to see how those concerns are currently expressed in the cross-curricular themes. Schools are now advised to consider air pollution, global warming, the destruction of the rainforests, the advance of deserts and the daily extinction of species (NCC, 1990e). This guidance is similar to Bellamy's analysis as long as one remembers that they describe the symptoms of environmental decline, not the causes or consequences. *Curriculum Guidance 7* offers clear and useful guidance on the aims, skills and knowledge which might be sued as starting points for school curricula. There is also a most useful analysis of inter-theme and National Curriculum subject links. Schools will need to continually review the relevance of the information used by pupils and teachers in their deliberations. For example, the issues causing most concern among some delegates at the Rio *Earth Summit* in 1992 were those of over-population causing excess pressure on resources; over-consumption by wealthy nations and Third World debt arising from those countries being persuaded to try and emulate market economy systems. The response of some western countries to those views is equally important when discussing these issues. While wanting to continue to advocate investigation in an historical perspective, schools will need increasingly to refer to contemporary information in order to help pupils reach informed decisions.

Environmental deterioration throws considerable doubt on views that citizenship education should foster group loyalty and white, middle-class values, especially in black and poor white neighbourhoods (Oldenquist, 1983 p.30–34) or that market economy systems have proved to be the most efficient means of production (Barrie, 1989). Consideration of environmental issues raises questions about the purpose of society, its value systems and how moral codes might be defined to guide decisions and carry individuals beyond personal considerations. Societies are faced by political uncertainty, threats to environmental stability of increasingly serious consequences and the re-emergence of nationalistic aspirations. An interaction could be developed between Marshall's process definition of citizenship, and environmental issues resulting in defining a state of being a *caring* citizen (Beehler, 1978). *Caring* citizenship means changing production methods to the sustainable use of resources to meet human need; it means government which all members of society recognise as being fair, just, accessible and tolerant of diverse cultures.

References

Barrie, N. (1989) Commission on Citizenship: *Paper presented to the Commission on Citizenship Seminar April 1989*, unpublished.

Beehler, R. (1978) *Moral Life: Values and Philosophical Enquiry*. Oxford: Basil Blackwell.

Dahrendorf, R. (1989) Commission on Citizenship: *Paper presented to the Commission on Citizenship Seminar April 1989*, unpublished.

42

Fogelman, K. (1991) 'Citizenship in Secondary Schools: The National Picture.' In Fogelman, K. (ed.) *Citizenship in Schools*. London: Fulton. p.35–48.

Gyte, G. and Hill, D. (1991) 'Citizenship in schools', in Fogelman, K. (ed.) *Citizenship in Schools*. London: Fulton.p.90.

Henderson, R. (1989) Commission on Citizenship: *Paper presented to the Commission on Citizenship Seminar April 1989*, unpublished.

Marshall, T.H. (1950) *Citizenship and Social Class*. Cambridge: Cambridge University Press.

Merton, T. (1970) *Raids on the Unspeakable*. New Directions: New York.

Morrell, F. (1991) 'The Work of the Speaker's Commission and its definition of Citizenship,' in Fogelman, K. (ed.) *Citizenship in Schools*. London: Fulton.

Oldenquist, A. (1980) 'On the nature of citizenship', *in Educational Leadership* **38**.

CHAPTER 5

Citizenship and Core and Foundation Subjects

MATHEMATICS

Rose Griffiths

Citizenship, with its emphasis on enabling children to become adults who play a full role in society, and with its messages of participation, rights and responsibilities, is a useful focus for reviewing the effectiveness of our maths teaching.

When I first started teaching maths, the method I used almost exclusively was the method by which I had been taught. I explained something to the whole class on the blackboard, worked through an example, and set some questions for the children to try themselves. I marked the children's books and set corrections, then started the process again, a few pages further forward in the text book. I worried about how to keep the class together, and how to keep up with the marking.

As I became more experienced as a teacher, I realised I had more cause to worry about why so many children only remembered what I had told them for a short time, so we had to keep repeating things year after year. And why were there so many children who could carry out quite complicated arithmetic, but floundered when given a problem in context? Exposition and standard algorithms might help children pass tests, but did not equip them effectively for the requirements of everyday life.

What mathematical knowledge and skills do people need, for home, school, work or leisure? The Cockcroft Committee pointed out that there is hardly any piece of mathematics which everyone uses, and its list of basic skills required is fairly short. But the report says very firmly: 'Most important of all is the need to have sufficient confidence to make effective use of whatever mathematical skill and understanding is possessed' (Cockcroft, 1982).

Sometimes, in the desire to link school mathematics to real life, I think teachers have fallen into three traps. One is the world of pseudo-reality, where, for example, you need to know the exact area of a room to buy carpet, and no-one expects you to pay for any of the pieces you don't use. Another is the trap of using contexts which are far too remote to be genuinely of interest, such as talking to children in Year 8 about bank loans. The third is almost the reverse difficulty: that we fail to deal with important issues because, perhaps, they seem too adult, and instead we only look at more trivial ones. For example, we spend time explaining and experimenting to see what a '1 in 4 chance' means in the context of a game but do not ever take that work a few steps further, to link it with more crucial uses of the phrase. The consequences of misunderstanding can be devastating – as for parents who interpreted '1 in 4' to mean that as their second child had a severe genetic disability, they could be certain that a third baby would not suffer from it.

How can we tell which real-life contexts will seem relevant to the students we work with? The answer is obviously to listen to them, to ask their opinion, and to try to put ourselves in their shoes. Children (and adults) who are not very confident about maths may find it particularly difficult to suggest questions they would like to consider, until they feel certain that we can be trusted not to make fun of them or let other students do so.

One very useful piece of work which arose from children's needs used an initial suggestion from our school's dinner supervisors. They had noticed that many children had exactly the same dinner each day, and were also concerned because children who received free meals were not using their full entitlement. The cafeteria system, with its requirement that you pay after collecting all your food, made many children feel anxious that they might spend too much, so they played safe, rather than risk their arithmetic letting them down. We discussed the problem with Year 7 children, and they decided to take action on three fronts: to provide better price labels and posters of sample menus for the dining room, to use copies of the price list to practice with in maths lessons, and to try to make up games which gave people practice in adding up the cost of their dinners. Motivation to help alleviate the problem was high, even amongst those who brought sandwiches. Children discussed the strategies they used for mental arithmetic, and we teachers were reassured by the quality and quantity of mathematics we saw going on. Most importantly, the children and the dinner ladies felt their work was successful.

A similar approach worked well with Year 9 children, on Ash (Action on Smoking and Health) Wednesday, after what felt like a complete failure in the previous school year to persuade any Year 9 children to consider the issues involved in a serious way. Instead of using 'Here is why you should not smoke' as our starting point, we posed the problem as it faced us: 'We want to persuade young people not to smoke. How can we do that? What methods will be most effective?' We gave the children the leaflets, posters

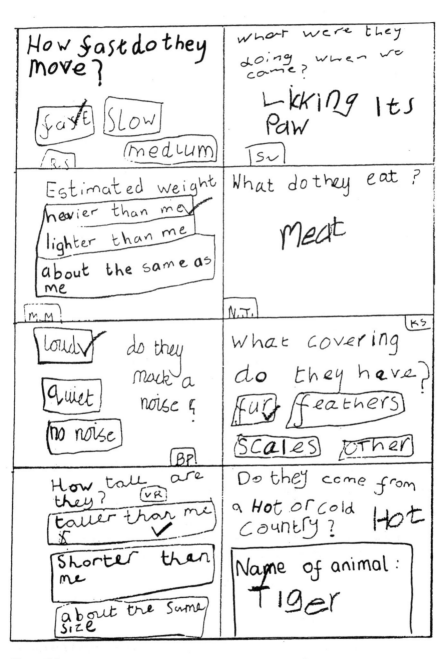

Figure 5.1

and handbooks full of statistics which we had received and talked about how an advertising team might work, sharing ideas, trying things out, and so on. By the end of the day we had posters, leaflets, lists, quizzes, scripts, charts and diagrams, but more importantly the majority of the students involved had spent time discussing, prioritising, and critically examining a wide range of statistical materials. And perhaps a few of them would think twice before lighting up...

Data handling is a key area of work for education for citizenship, and it is one where younger children can gain a great deal from being given more responsibility and control. A Year 2 and 3 class who had spent some time collecting and analysing data about fruit and then about teachers ('What is your favourite food?' 'What are your hobbies?') were given the task of designing a data collection sheet to use for the animals they were going to visit at the zoo. On visits with previous classes, Anne, their teacher, had drawn up a worksheet herself for children to complete, but felt the children spent more time copying answers from each other's sheets than they did on finding things out for themselves. This time, Anne asked the children to begin by writing lists of questions which they might want to ask about the animals, then by group and next by whole-class discussion (and a vote if need be) they agreed upon a selection of questions which were printed and used on the trip. Some questions were commuted for ones which would be easier to answer ('What are their hobbies?' became 'What were they doing when we came?'), and some were discarded because not many children wanted to know the answer to them. The sheets were very successful because the children were so confident about using them, and they wanted to collect the information to bring it back to school to use it (see figure 5.1.)

People's needs and interests have always been the impetus for new mathematics to be developed. Perhaps we should make better use of the history of maths, telling stories to explain why people came to agreements about the rules and conventions we use today, or how they developed new ideas. In a world which is changing fast, a feeling of continuity is important.

The mathematics we use with children should make sense to them, because it is useful or interesting or beautiful. As the report, *Better Mathematics*, says: 'For Mathematical activity to be meaningful, it needs to be personally fulfilling' (Ahmed, 1987). Sometimes it may be obviously and directly linked to real-life purposes, sometimes to more abstract ones. Most importantly, we should teach it in ways which make children feel confident, which give them some control over and responsibility for what they do.

References

Ahmed, A. et al (1987) *Better Mathematics: a Curriculum Development Study*. London: HMSO.

Cockcroft, W.H. (Chairman) (1982) *Mathematics Counts: report of the Committee of Enquiry*. London: HMSO.

SCIENCE

Jenny Harrison

Impressions of science amongst the public stem from experiences at school and from images, often negative ones, reflected in the media. To enable pupils today to become willing, active, and effective participators in a society which is inherently scientific and technological means overcoming suspicions of science and developing constructive attitudes to the work of scientists. The following paragraphs provide some insight into what it means to be scientific, together with a consideration of possible styles of teaching and learning which can be adopted in science lessons in order to reinforce the principles of citizenship.

Being 'good at science' involves both knowing and doing. A major contribution of science to the curriculum is to allow understanding of key scientific concepts and their technological applications. Another important contribution is to allow first-hand experiences of scientific methods of investigation, disciplined enquiries, and relevant problem-solving. The whole of Attainment Target 1 on Scientific Investigation provides for the increasing independence of pupils and enables the teacher to become facilitator as well as imparter of knowledge. Such active learning gives pupils responsibility for planning, organisation and evaluation of their own learning. Practical skills, such as taking measurements, need not become simply ends in themselves. For instance, when pupils gather information from various woodland sites on plant density, soil depth, pH, and light intensity they could be asked to determine which factors are associated with a particular plant species, and could then question factors likely to be influential in determining the presence and growth of the species under study. In this way they learn to draw conclusions supported by the results, to consider possible sources of error in gathering their data, and to decide whether there are other influential factors affecting conditions at the chosen sites. Opportunities have then been created for pupils not only to understand more about scientific ways of working but also to develop attitudes which can respect evidence, tolerate uncertainty, give honest reports and critically appraise information.

Co-operative structures can also be built into the lessons. It is common for pupils to work during practical sessions in pairs or larger groups and genuine group work is only achieved when there is collaboration and a common purpose. Pupils can be encouraged to work in groups of differing sizes and composition, with people they do not know or perhaps do not even like. There are opportunities, too, for peer teaching, through presentations of practical data and reports, and for peer testing of skills such as the correct use of a chemical balance.

It is in this area of personal development that science education can make another vital contribution to the curriculum. At best, it should be arousing interest and curiosity by selecting meaningful everyday contexts and encouraging pupils to ask questions, suggest ideas and make predictions. It should encourage responsible attitudes towards health and safety by involving pupils in negotiating codes of behaviour in a potentially dangerous science laboratory. Such strategies require teachers to be willing and able to question just what pupils are experiencing in their lessons and to present science as an essentially human activity. For example through the study of water and air pollution in the environment, or the study of velocity and acceleration and its application to adequate braking distances and the required use of seat belts, science becomes less remote from people's lives. Considerable responsibility can also be given to pupils for the care and welfare of a wildlife area, or the fish tank in the school entrance, thereby encouraging pupils to respect living organisms and the physical environment.

The social aims of science education have been appreciated for many years. Bernal (1946) wrote that science education should 'provide enough understanding of the place of science in society to enable the great majority that will not be actively engaged in scientific pursuits to collaborate intelligently with those that are and be able to criticise or appreciate the affect of science on society'. Sir George Porter (1986) clarified this when he stated, 'Science makes change possible – everyone needs to be in a fit state to judge whether we want that change.' Thus amongst the list of scientific attitudes which need developing in all science lessons, and summarised by Jennings (1983), is an 'appreciation of the limitations of science and respect for other forms of knowledge'; another is the 'recognition that social problems even those that are science related, cannot be solved by scientific means alone.' The NC Working Group for Science (DES, 1987) had as one of its aims for children 'to gain balanced insights into the importance of science and technology in the economy and to the quality of life of all citizens.' In the *Non-statutory Guidance to the Science NC* (1989), it is stated that part of the contribution that science makes to the curriculum is to 'encourage pupils to develop a sense of their responsibilities as members of society and of the contributions they can make to it' and also to appreciate that 'moral and ethical issues raised by developing technology can bring added awareness of the wider issues and difficulties involved in the application of science in the developing and developed world'.

By confronting issues of a controversial nature we enable pupils to form opinions and beliefs, and to have existing ones challenged and reformed. They can debate 'respect for life' versus the advantages of animal dissection, and the implications for personal choice and freedom of mass screening of immigrants using genetic fingerprinting techniques. The challenge for teachers is to create a climate in which they can listen to what the pupils say, allow pupils to express an opinion, and provide the time for such reflection. Joan Solomon (1989) argues a powerful case for *discussion* to be part of science education. There are excellent strategies for this type of work in the DISS Project (Discussion of Issues in School Science Project) and in other Science, Technology and Society courses. Some start with a historical study, and then look at how the topics affect us today. Pupils are encouraged to contribute their own ideas about society's needs and values. The Science and Technology in Society (SATIS) materials (Holman, 1986) aim to relate science to its social and technological context, using controversial issues, group discussions, role-play, problem-solving and reading activities. Here are many attempts to show the relevance of science and to humanise science in ways which can be woven into the fabric of science lessons.

Practical field activities are frequently used to make scientific phenomena more real through experience, but beyond the experiential aspects of the visit to the local quarry, or the environmental project on pollution indicators in a school pond, there are more far-reaching aims. These can involve pupils in planning and organising a day off-site, in joining a school science club, in an active campaign to maintain or improve the school environment, in classroom displays of visual material, as well as providing opportunities to go out into the community or indeed to bring the community into the school.

There are opportunities too for emphasizing ethnic and cultural diversity in our society by careful choice of different social contexts for topics such as diet and nutrition, energy, or examples of ecosystems. The white, eurocentric images of science have been all too common in many classroom activities in the past. Similarly, much has been written on ways of encouraging girls to take up the physical sciences (Kelly, 1987). The focus of many studies has been on changing classroom practices and teacher attitudes, emphasizing the development of an atmosphere of mutual respect, trust, community, of shared leadership, and looking for ways of integrating feelings and ideas in science. It is known that girls become more involved if their own perspectives on problems, issues and ideas can be articulated in the lessons. It is clear that a lack of personal scientific knowledge results in a sense of powerlessness and inaction but if, as well as knowledge, a sense of self esteem, and of belonging to the classroom culture can be encouraged, 'citizen science' will go some way to removing the cold and clinical image of science, by presenting it in the context of a caring and responsible society.

References

Holman, J. (1986) *Science and Technology in Science* . Hatfield: A.S.E.

Bernal, J.D. (1946) 'Science teaching in general education,' *School Science Review*, **27**, p.150–158.

Jennings, A. (1983) 'Biological Education,' *Journal of Biological Education*, **17**(4), p.298–302.

Kelly, A. (1987) *Science for Girls* . Milton Keynes: Open University Press.

50

Porter, G. (1986) 'What is science for?' *New Scientist*, Vol **112** No. 1535, p.32–34.
Solomon, J. (1989) 'Social Construction of School Science,' in Millar, R. (ed.) *Doing Science: Images of Science in Science Education*, London: Falmer Press.

ENGLISH

Ros McCulloch

Curriculum Guidance 8, in enumerating citizenship topics, mentions English as relevant to 30 out of the 32 items. In its correlation between the citizenship curriculum and the National Curriculum, and suggestions for activities, English attainment targets are being met at all Key Stages. English is thus a central, if not the central, component in the development of citizenship, and indeed it is not hard to see why this should be so. There is a consensus among English teachers that, in their classrooms, activities and contexts should be provided within which pupils can develop their capacities as readers, writers, speakers and listeners. Because it is primarily through language that we exchange information in all spheres of human life, it is in this subject above all that our pupils can explore and experiment with central themes of citizenship in group and individual settings.

The contexts within which the National Curriculum requires these linguistic capacities to be developed are various: they can be public and formal (composing a letter to one's MP, talking to the Head); or personal and informal (persuading a parent to give you more pocket money, negotiating the difficulties of friendship). However, in focusing upon the use of language, whether spoken or written, pupils are being urged first to distinguish, then to produce, those forms most appropriate to particular situations. Thus, the effective writer or speaker has her/his cause taken up, or avoids censure, while the good persuader gets the rise in pocket money, or keeps the friendship intact. Pupils thus come to see that language has consequences in the world, and that to increase one's mastery of forms of language is to increase one's capacity for being an effective agent in the world.

The English classroom, with its working and reworking of such contexts, mediates between the pupils' increasing confidence in language mastery and the real world, by providing a laboratory where experiment and improvement can take place. In this way, working with a wide range of communications materials, presented in a variety of media, pupils begin to develop a critical awareness of language processes. This might be more fully explained by the notion of the reflexiveness of language. In assessing the activities of the English classroom, teachers and pupils are considering successful language models which can be re-used or adapted; or they are examining unsuccessful ones to see how messages were misinterpreted, or otherwise rendered ineffective. Language is itself the medium for reflecting critically upon language, so that pupils begin to work out for themselves the rules for effective communication through processes of trial, error and reflection.

Developing this thought, we might argue further that pupils engaged in this kind of critical reflection in the English classroom, coming to an awareness of language that enables them to understand its processes and consequences, are developing another critical capacity. They come to see how language can be used by others to persuade, or even manipulate them; pupils thus empowered have the opportunity to develop much more fully as individual and social beings, and, potentially, as citizens. Indeed, it is difficult to see what content the notion of an active citizen could have at all without significant communication skills, skills developed above all in the English classroom.

The development of these competences is of course morally neutral: communication skills can be used for base ends as easily as for virtuous ones, so I would want to argue more strongly that, as a normative force, the English classroom has much to offer the development of central themes of citizenship.

Although as we have seen, *Curriculum Guidance 8* frequently mentions English, it is primarily as a framework for language activities. It is rather muted on the role of literature in the development of citizenship, confining itself to the mention of stories such as 'The tiger who came to tea' and 'The Three Little Pigs' at Key Stage 1. Yet literature, surely, has a far larger part to play than this. Part of the successful development of citizenship in the pupil lies in her/his ability to 'develop a personal moral code and to explore values and beliefs. Shared values, such as concern for others...as well as moral qualities such as honesty and truthfulness, should be promoted.' (*Curriculum Guidance 8*, p. 4)

From the evidence collected by Burkimsher and Vlaeminke (1991) in a range of schools, schools feel the main elements of citizenship education lie in the notions of ethos/ambience/values/attitudes rather than in the accumulation in pupils' heads of facts about voting rights and the like. Ethos and ambience are of course bound up with school values and attitudes – how a school speaks to its senior people, its pupils, its cleaners. Burkimsher has further commented (at a conference organised by CSCS in Leicester on November 16th 1991) that he finds children themselves to have a highly developed sense of fairness and justice. Schools can of course foster this by appropriate behavioural policies and through school activities, since it is after all in the impact of events upon us that we feel most keenly the force of fairness or unfairness, justice or injustice. However, we cannot expose children to all the possible complexities of such moral experiences (nor would we wish to). We need therefore to explore other ways of extending children's awareness of justice, as well as other moral values (charity, compassion, respect for persons) and in this way fulfil the demands of the citizenship curriculum.

I would argue that it is in the English classroom that the variety of human experience can be explored, and the parameters of moral actions discussed, more effectively than in any other subject, and I would suggest that this is so because of the **particularity** and **participativeness** that literature *of all sorts* offers.

My point is a simple one. Where other socially investigative subjects like Sociology and Politics deal with general rules or events affecting large numbers of (usually nameless) persons, literature – books, stories, films – deals with particular persons in particular places having particular things happen to them. It is with particularity that we most identify (as every Charity Appeal knows) since our empathic tendency is to identify with the lives of people whose stories draw us in. Sometimes readers' involvement in fictional characters blurs the edges of reality – Richardson's audience for *Clarissa* was only the first in an honourable line of devotees who today petition the writers of *The Archers*, *East Enders* and *Coronation Street*, trying to prevent authors from making nasty things happen to their favourite characters.

The skilful English teacher, however, will encourage children to engage with, but also to preserve a sense of detachment from, the characters in a story, and will do this through the characteristic activities of the English classroom – Did you feel X was right to do this? How did you feel when Y said that? Can you think of reasons why Z reacted as she did? What would you have done in situation S? All these questions urge pupils to make the story their own, by developing their personal response to the actions, values and attitudes that the story has presented to them. But in doing that they probe their own moral values – what is fair, what is appropriate, how people should be treated, what people's responsibilities are, what they are entitled to. These questions, crucially concerned with the development of a personal code of values, are surely at the heart of citizenship.

References

Burkimsher, M. and Vlaeminke, M. (1991) 'Approaches to Citizenship' in Fogelman K. (ed.) *Citizenship in Schools*. London: Fulton.

HISTORY

David Kerr

There is a long tradition of links between history and citizenship education (or civics) in British education (Batho, 1990; Brown, 1991). History is often a central component in citizenship education. The link is based on the overlap between the aims and purposes of history and of citizenship in the curriculum. The association is complex because the reasons advanced for studying history and developing citizenship education in schools are constantly changing, influenced by the spirit of the age and prevailing ideas about education. As a result, the nature of the link between history and citizenship education in the curriculum has shifted over the past two centuries.

For example, in Victorian times education was openly for social purposes. The aim of citizenship education was to ensure that pupils understood their position in society and accompanying duties. History teaching supported this aim. The lessons learnt from studying famous people and the growth of British government and empire confirmed to pupils their position and duties within society.

By the 1920s, under the impact of the First World War, the cornerstone of education was 'interest', particularly individual interest in the national and local community. Citizenship education sought to inform pupils about human relations and relate it to their social environment. History was central to this through the insights it gave into human nature and actions.

History teaching encouraged discussion and personal experience to explore local and national events. Indeed Helen Madeley in her influential book *History as a School of Citizenship* argued that 'if History is to survive, it must serve the ends of citizenship.' (Madeley, 1920).

By the 1960s the emphasis in education had shifted to social studies. Citizenship education had broadened from national and local concerns to developing an awareness of world citizenship and the economic aspects of life. History was deemed less appropriate for this. Instead citizenship education became associated with the new social sciences, such as politics, sociology and economics, which specifically dealt with human society and social relationships.

It is vital for history teachers to examine the tradition of links when considering the association between history and citizenship education in the National Curriculum. The examination is important for two reasons. First, to alert teachers that the guidance for history (DES, 1991) and citizenship (NCC, 1990f) in the National Curriculum is value-laden. It is an historical product; the latest in the series of definitions of the aims and purpose of school history and citizenship education. It is influenced by the spirit of the age and prevailing educational objectives. Teachers need to use their professional judgement to interpret the guidance and decide how best to approach it. There is a fine line between education and indoctrination.

The second reason is to enable teachers to recognise the relationship between definitions of school history and citizenship education and approaches to teaching and learning. The reasons advanced for studying history and developing citizenship education invariably govern attitudes as to what is taught (the subject matter) and how it is taught (the method of study and approach to the subject matter). They also determine the outcomes of the intended learning. It is the debate about purpose and process which conspires to make history such a controversial subject and citizenship education such a contentious issue in the curriculum. This is the case worldwide (Gross and Dynneson, 1990). It is no coincidence that the guidance documents for history and citizenship have provoked fierce debate (Heater, 1991 and Slater, 1991). The link between history and citizenship education is as much about purpose and process as content.

The National Curriculum has given renewed impetus to the links between history and citizenship and restored history as a central component of citizenship education. There is intentional overlap in aims and purpose between the guidance for history and for citizenship. Commander Saunders Watson, in his letter to the Secretary of State introducing the History Working Group's Interim Report (DES, 1989), declared that their aim had been 'to devise a course of school history which will equip pupils with the historical knowledge, understanding and skills to enable them to play their part as informed citizens of the twenty-first century', while the Report emphasises that 'History is a vital element within the curriculum for the education of citizens'. This message is reinforced by the many examples of links to history in the guidance for citizenship.

Closer examination of the guidance for citizenship reveals the considerable overlap with history in the knowledge, understanding, skills and attitudes to be developed and the approach to learning. The eight components of citizenship education – including work, employment, leisure, family and community – are the lifeblood of the programmes of study in history. History offers a unique opportunity to put these components in historical context and help pupils to understand the present in the light of the past.

The approach to learning in the guidance document and its aim are equally familiar to history teachers. Citizenship education is centred on the interpretation of evidence and the formation of conclusions based on evidence, often concerning controversial issues. The aim is to help pupils to develop skills and attitudes in handling evidence – including detecting bias and omission, respecting evidence, clarifying their own values and tolerating different points of view – which are transferable to adult life. This is the aim of learning through the three attainment targets (ATs) in the National Curriculum for History.

There is sufficient overlap in the guidance to suggest that citizenship education can be integrated as part of learning in history in many contexts. The central question is how can that learning in history best equip pupils with the understanding, skills and attitudes to be informed citizens? It is not enough to assume that pursuing the history ATs will prepare pupils for their roles and responsibilities as citizens. Integration will only be successful if history teachers think through the implications of developing citizenship education as a natural part of the process of learning in history in their classroom.

History can assist best through a process of learning that helps pupils to develop a critical respect for evidence. Above all, it includes helping pupils to appreciate that different interpretations of citizenship and its components in history lead to different questions and alternative ways of seeing things. It requires careful thought and planning in each context. There are a number of steps history teachers might take to develop this process:

(1) Identify the scope that particular areas of history provide for appropriate *contexts* for integrating components of Citizenship Education as part of learning in History;
(2) Establish, for those areas, lesson intentions to help pupils to achieve the ATs in History through particular *activities*;
(3) *Resource* the lessons and identify appropriate *teacher* interventions for learning;
(4) *Assess* the outcomes in terms of pupils' understanding in modern contexts.

This might work as follows:

(1) **Context.** The teacher recognises that nineteenth century industrial Britain offers the possibility of investigating the law and citizens through the context of the case of the Tolpuddle Martyrs.
(2) **Activities.** The teacher designs activities to get pupils
    – to form opinions, from a variety of sources on the Tolpuddle case (AT3), about the relationship between the law and citizens and in the process investigate how interpretations are related to the selection and use of resources (AT2).
    – to compare those opinions with their views about the law and citizens in modern Britain.
(3) **Resources and Teaching.** The teacher selects a range of sources showing different interpretations of the Tolpuddle case. S/he ascertains pupil ideas about the law and citizens, for these ideas affect the way pupils approach the historical context and the evidence presented to them. The teacher turns these ideas back to pupils to enable them to review their own thinking about the law and citizen rights and responsibilities.
(4) **Assessment.** The teacher introduces sources with different views of the modern legal system to ascertain how far pupils are able to transfer the knowledge, understanding and skills developed in the historical context to a modern one.

This is not an easy process to develop. It is vital if learning in history is to equip pupils with the historical knowledge, understanding and skills to become informed citizens. It is a learning process which encourages pupils to develop a critical analysis of society and the concept of the citizen within it. Who knows, it may persuade some of them to contribute to future definitions of history and citizenship education.

And so the tradition goes on...

References

Batho, G. (1990) 'The history of the teaching of civics and citizenship in English schools', *The Curriculum Journal*, **1**(1), p. 92–100.

Brown, C. (1991) 'Education for Citizenship – old wine in new bottles?', *Citizenship* **1**(2), p. 6–9.

Department of Education and Science (1989) *Interim Report of the History Working Group*. London: HMSO.

Department of Education and Science (1991) *History in the National Curriculum*. London: HMSO.

Gross, R.E. and Dynneson, T.L. (1990) *Social Science Perspectives on Citizenship Education*. New York: Teachers College Press.

Heater, D. (1991) 'What is Citizenship?", *Citizenship*, **1**(2), p.3.

Madeley, H.M. (1920) *History as a School of Citizenship*. Oxford: Oxford University Press.

Slater, J. (1991) 'History in the national curriculum: the Final Report of the History Working Group' in Aldrich, R. (ed.) *History in the National Curriculum*. London: Kogan Page.

GEOGRAPHY

Patrick Bailey

Geography addresses the central concerns and issues of citizenship education directly. Citizenship education explains why society can only work to the benefit of everybody if all its members act with consideration towards others. The central message of geography complements this: it is that all human beings are dependent upon one another because all share an environment which is globally inter-connected. What people do in one place can therefore affect people, even in faraway places. An extreme case: those who decide to detonate an atomic bomb will affect everyone on earth because all breathe the same global atmosphere and drink from the one global water supply. Geography also teaches the absolute dependence of everyone, even supermarket shoppers, upon the natural world and reminds us that the delicate balances of that world may easily be upset.

Both geography and citizenship education arise from the experience of the child growing up. Both are ways of ordering the child's experience and of drawing useful conclusions from that ordering. The very young child soon realises that the home environment is both social and spatial. (It is, of course, also set in time, and this realisation is the beginning of history). The spatial environment is found to have size, shape and boundaries and it has to be shared with others. Parts of it indeed may be 'owned' by others. Other people determine how different parts of space can be used; some places and areas prove more suitable than others for certain activities. So gradually the child's perceived environment takes shape and extends into the wider spaces beyond the family. Normally the child learns to live in this expanding environment with increasing freedom and independence; unless, that is, the environment is stultified by fear, hatred, disease, drought and famine, as it is for many children today.

In a well-ordered family the growing child soon learns lessons which also apply to world society: that if all members are to prosper they must practise

- give and take in the use of resources;
- care and conservation rather than destructive exploitation of what is available;
- collaboration instead of unbridled competition;
- giving help where help is needed.

Geography and citizenship education together teach us about the conditions for a harmonious, humane family and for a harmonious, humane world. They also remind us that these conditions are established first where one happens to be. A central message of geography is that responsible citizenship begins at home.

Citizenship and Geography's Five Attainment Targets

The National Curriculum regulations for geography (DES 1991) divide the subject into five related parts, termed Attainment Targets (ATs). These targets are not intended to be syllabus headings; they are divisions of convenience for assessment purposes. All five sub-divisions offer possibilities for making links with citizenship education, as follows.

AT 1 Geographical skills

The skills specific to geography are mainly those relating to making, using and interpreting maps. There are also the skills of interpreting photographs and graphical presentations, linked with the handling of simple statistics. Maps are essential tools for making sense of social and economic information in one's own town, and maps, tables of statistical data and photographs make ideal starts for citizenship discussions. Topics such as the nature of inner city decline and possibilities for regeneration at once suggest themselves.

In addition, geography lessons make use of all the general learning skills listed on pages 3–4 of *Education for Citizenship* (NCC, 1990f). Investigatory and reporting skills are especially important; this is because geography is a 'finding out' subject. All geography begins with somebody somewhere, going out to discover what some aspect of the world is like and why. The geographical approach is to observe, record, assemble information into usable forms, pose and test hypotheses, draw conclusions, present findings. This approach lies at the centre of geographical education and begins with the youngest children. Such investigatory methods give ample scope for collaborative work, the discussion of ideas and information and the development of oral, visual and written presentations, all citizenship skills.

AT2 Place knowledge and understanding

This important AT is designed to ensure that young people leave school with a systematised knowledge of the configurations of their own country and of the world. It is necessary to possess an outline knowledge of Britain in order to decide where to look for work, where to try to locate a business, where to go for holidays. At the world scale, a basic knowledge of the relative positions, sizes, populations and resources of continents and important countries is part of the equipment of any competent citizen.

The world after the Cold War demands better world-wide place knowledge than ever before, if only because the political monoliths of that dark period are breaking up into small units, each pursuing its own policies. Situations which call for citizens to respond in informed ways to world events seem likely to multiply. An increasing number of United Nations interventions in world affairs will call for the support of informed citizens in member states, willing to pay higher taxes. One of geography's most important tasks at present is to provide those citizens with their information base.

AT 3 Physical geography

The main message of this AT is that the conditions of the natural world are produced and maintained by natural processes, working together in complicated, finely balanced systems; and that these processes affect us all.

Citizens in an urban society such as ours urgently need reminding that, like the desert nomad or the traditional farmer in Africa, we depend upon the atmosphere, soil, water and the 'web of life' of which we are all part. This AT provides a balanced account of the major processes at work upon the earth's surface, a necessary foundation for all work in human and environmental geography.

AT 4 Human geography

This AT explores the ways in which human beings occupy and utilise the earth's surface. It looks at settlement, farming, town development, industries, communication and transport networks, energy sources and the exchange of materials, goods and services. It also considers the migration of peoples within and between continents and countries and the consequences of such migrations. There are many ways of forging citizenship links through this AT. For instance, almost any industrial study will bring out Britain's dependence upon world trade, the concern of every citizen. Similarly, studies of British farms show how land use depends as much upon world markets and subsidies from the government and the EC as upon soil quality and climate.

Human geography gives many opportunities for investigations by individuals and groups, for debates and the arguing of cases, for the evaluation of evidence. Inevitably it also raises ethical questions, considerations of the rightness of what is being done.

AT 5 Environmental geography

This fifth AT brings studies in physical and human geography together. It shows how attempts to intervene in natural environments must take proper account of the processes at work in those environments, otherwise disaster may ensue. Examples of such disasters include the creation of the 'dust bowls' of the North American prairie and parts of central Asia and the drying up of the Aral Sea.

The modern industrial world causes environmental damage on an unprecedented scale. If citizens are to press governments to put matters right (and it is urgent that they do so), they have to understand what responsible environmental management entails and be willing to pay for it. Here also the lessons of citizenship and geography are complementary.

Fifty years ago, Ernest Hemingway wrote a powerful novel about the Spanish Civil War, called *For Whom the Bell Tolls.* In it he predicted that the evil powers unleased in that war would shortly pursue their ambitions on a wider stage than Spain; and that therefore what was happening to Spanish children, men and women was everyone's concern. So it turned out to be. He prefaced his book with a quotation from John Donne's *Devotions*:

> No man is an **Iland**, intire of itself; every man is a peece of the **Continent**, a part of the **maine**... any man's **death** diminishes **me**, because I am involved in **Mankinde**...

That is the message of both geography and citizenship education.

References

DES (1991) *Geography in the National Curriculum.* London: DES.
NCC (1991) *Geography: non-statutory guidance.* York: NCC.

DESIGN AND TECHNOLOGY

Tina Jarvis

Technology is an essential part of human culture because it is concerned with achievement of a wide range of human purposes (Black and Harrison, 1985). It involves finding effective ways of providing food, water, warmth, shelter, security, clothing, health and opportunities for interacting with others in order to improve day-to-day survival. As societies develop so these refinements are more related to enriching the quality of life.

Technological products cannot be divorced from the culture or society for which they are produced since each product is created to solve a specific need for a particular location, taking into account available resources and skills. Consequently what is good technology in one place may not be appropriate in another. Thus house building in Greenland, Tokyo and England use quite different technologies. Indeed there have been disasters when one technology is transferred from one society to another unchanged, as in the introduction of European agricultural systems into the different ecosystems of Australia and West Africa.

What is perceived as a problem in technology will also depend on each society which additionally sets the limits on the kinds of solutions that can be seriously entertained; sets the limits of what capital, resources and time will be made available to solve the problem; and scrutinises those that are tried (Jarvie, 1967). The technologies of clean air and auto safety, for example, were not problems which concerned society a century ago and the method for solving widely recognised environmental problems, such as the rapid denudation of the rainforests, is restricted by the priorities of each country and society.

Technology has been seen as a panacea for all human problems. It has been assumed that such problems as lack of food to feed the world's growing population, increased pollution, depletion of energy resources, and disease will eventually be solved through technological innovation. Technology can indeed go a long way towards these goals but each development creates changes in society which almost inevitably create other challenges. Technological development involves achieving acceptable compromises rather than perfect solutions.

Citizens must become more aware of the way technology affects society by changing the home, work-place, and life-styles. They should appreciate its great power and their responsibility to challenge and alter it through personal action and use of their democratic right to vote and express their views. Citizens need to understand technology to be able to predict the effects of introducing new systems or processes, appreciate the restrictions on what particular technologies may achieve, identify problems for which technologies might provide solutions (Medway, 1989), and appreciate the limits and possibilities of technology to bring about an improved quality of life and/or increased harm to life on this planet (Bybee, 1985). It is essential, therefore, that young people develop technological competency alongside skills and attitudes of good citizenship.

Relating the Technology National Curriculum and education for citizenship

The Technology National Curriculum outlines a process which includes observation and evaluation of existing situations to identify needs and opportunities for improvement. The ways to achieve these are explored, planned and implemented. The success of action is evaluated in terms of costs, which include financial, time involved and effect on others. The task may be fairly basic, for example making a working toy for nursery children, or more complex, such as considering the issues of building an industrial estate in a green belt area. In each case action will often create further needs or difficulties to be overcome, and so the cycle continues.

Problem solving

Technology thus enables pupils to learn to tackle such tasks in an effective manner, considering a range of solutions, planning effectively, applying knowledge and skills to use a wide variety of materials and tools, and constantly reviewing and improving their approach. The skill of problem solving is also essential to good citizenship (NCC, 1990f p.4). Additionally, many design and technology projects are concerned with evaluating and developing products in the community, business and industry, such as providing artefacts to help disabled or old people, designing play provision for the young, improving library facilities, evaluating retail facilities and suggesting ways to improve the local environment. These enable pupils to explore some of the essential contexts for citizenship (NCC, 1990f p.5–9) in components such as Community, Work, Employment and Leisure and Public Services in particular. Other positive attitudes of independence, cooperation and consideration for others – which are essential if pupils are to value democracy and its associated duties, responsibilities and rights – are also developed through design and technology activities throughout the primary and secondary school.

Independence

For young people to acquire the technological skills of identifying needs for themselves, develop their creativity, adapt, respond to problems and mistakes, and evaluate their own work they must be involved in some of the decisions regarding what they make or do. These might be related to the day-to-day running of the class, for instance:

- helping to decide how to set up a central storage area for tools and materials;

- considering how to reduce litter in the grounds;
- making suggestions to extend other curricular subjects, e.g. making model period furniture after a visit to a historical house.

Alternatively, once a task has been decided, a non-prescriptive approach will ensure that pupils make decisions for themselves on the method, equipment to use or detail of the product. They will inevitably make mistakes and have to contend with them, albeit under the guidance of the teacher. Such activities provide the opportunity to help young people become independent, thinking adults who are more likely to regard difficult tasks as challenges than as barriers.

Working together

Cooperation and sensitivity concerning the needs of others are fostered, and indeed need to to be taught, because technology requires that pupils understand and design organisational systems as well as work in teams, share tasks and take leadership roles during the development of different products. Discussing and teaching collaborative and leadership skills, including helping the pupils to identify rules for behaviour and methods for optimising problem-solving with many opportunities to practice these skills in the safe environment of the school, must assist development of appropriate behaviour of the adult citizen.

An understanding and appreciation of different cultures

The Technology National Curriculum specifically requires pupils not only to consider their own needs and those of their peers, but also to evaluate and create products for people from a variety of backgrounds and cultures. In order to devise appropriate products for parents, old age pensioners, individuals with disabilities and people of different cultures it is important to try to empathise with their requirements. Technology education can thus widen the cultural base of school studies, so that the technologies of non-Europeans can be understood as cultural answers to the problems confronting a particular society (Cosgrove, 1990). For example, when pupils study homes, clothes, methods of food preparation, diets and religious buildings, if they understand that each product is a logical response to factors such as available materials, climate and social requirements they may be less inclined to criticise or dismiss the lifestyle of others, and by doing so hopefully become more tolerant and understanding.

Conflicts of interests

Throughout the primary and secondary school, technological activities can demonstrate that actions affect others, possibly detrimentally, and that every individual has responsibility to look for creative compromises that protect and care for the environment and others in society. When designing a park, pupils can be helped to see that the needs of very young children may not coincide with the requirements of elderly people or those with physical disabilities. By using visits, role play and discussions older children can explore a greater variety of conflicts between individuals or groups of people; between long term and short term interests; and between economic progress and the need to protect the Earth's limited resources. For example, Littledyke (1989) outlines a project for upper juniors in which children took on roles of the inhabitants in an imaginary village community where the environmental quality of life was high but where many people experienced unemployment. Plans to build an agrochemical reprocessing plant were then introduced. As the children acted out their response, in role, to this news, they identified the benefits of more jobs and increased opportunities for local business compared to the possible damage and disturbance to the village.

Conclusion

Technological literacy becomes an enabler of good citizenship – a correlate of social responsibility (Lewis and Gagel, 1992) and assists the citizen as decision-maker in a democratic society (Fleming, 1989). This is reflected in the Design and Technology National Curriculum which has the potential to help create imaginative, thinking, tolerant and responsible adults better able to adapt and cope with day-to-day problems and aware of the effect of their actions with sufficient knowledge and confidence not to abdicate their responsibilities.

References

Black, P. and Harrison, G. (1985) *In Place of Confusion: Technology and Science in the School Curriculum. A discussion paper*. Nottingham: Nuffield Curriculum Trust & National Centre for School Technology, Trent Polytechnic.

Bybee, R. (1985) 'The restoration of confidence in science and technology education', *School Science and Mathematics*, **85** (2), 95–108.

Cosgrove, M. (1990) *Hands and Brains: Working paper 90.4:* Science and Education Research Group. Sydney: University of Technology.

Fleming, R. (1989) 'Literacy for a technological age,' *Science Education*, **73**(4), 391–404.

Jarvie, I. (1967) 'Technology and the structure of knowledge' in Mitcham, C. and Mackey, R. (eds) (1972) *Philosophy and Technology*. New York: Free Press.

Lewis, T. and Gagel, C. (1992) 'Technological literacy: a critical analysis', *Journal of Curriculum Studies*, **24**(2), 117–138.

Littledyke, M. (1989) 'Employment versus pollution', *Questions*, **2**(3) 8–9.

Medway, P. (1989) 'Issues in the theory and practice of technological education', *Studies in Science Education*, **16**, 1–24.

LANGUAGES

Richard Aplin

In the first thirty years after the Second World War, the teaching of Modern Languages in Britain was in danger of becoming something of a marginal activity. Marginal because of its traditionally exclusive position in the curriculum offered by selective schools and in the academic streams of wider ability schools (at least in early forms of comprehensive reorganisation). Marginal because of its perceived elitist character, connected as it traditionally was to its role in the education of the upper echelons of society. Marginal because of its retention of a model of native speaker perfection against which every learner attempt was doomed to inadequacy, and by its insistence on a rigorous method of excluding those who thus failed, with a brutality redolent of Passchendaele. Marginal because of its content's exotic irrelevance to the perceived needs of its learners As a result, generations of, by its standards, successful learners still find themselves unable to make use of their 'school French' which has become a kind of accepted code for the apparent linguistic incompetence of the British.

Yet by September 1992, the study of a 'Modern Foreign Language' (a term adopted by the Department of Education and Science from the late 1980s) has become an integral part of the National Curriculum in the secondary phase and is included as a Foundation Subject for all pupils in Key Stages 3 and 4. The model of performance adopted is one which stresses skills of communication in rather than knowledge about a language. A radical move dating from the mid-1970s to overcome the failure of modern language teaching to meet the needs of all learners (Page, 1974; HMI, 1977; Page & Hewett, 1987) revitalised the way of assessing progress by means of graded objectives and recognising what pupils are able to do rather than asserting their failure to be foreign. Connected with the growth of graded objectives and assessment, a revamp of syllabus content, firmly founded on linguistic theories of functions of language and on the perceived needs of learners (Van Ek, 1977) allowed the introduction of GCSE in languages to be a fundamental shift from the inappropriateness of what went before.

The reasons for this dramatic and rapid change in fortune and status for languages teaching partly stem from a determination by practitioners to address the challenge of the comprehensive school, but are also largely driven by a public awareness of the inadequate linguistic performance by the British in an international context. The most powerful influence on this awareness has come from a sustained official campaign emphasising the importance of language proficiency in securing overseas markets, so that a vision of languages combined with business skills has rapidly become a shibboleth of the 1990s. The growing acceptance of Britain's place in the European Community, and the congruence of the UK presidency in late 1992 with the full introduction of the Single European Market have given a particular impetus to the rising expectations of languages teachers. Policies such as a move towards a diversification of foreign languages in schools (Dickson and Lee, 1990) and proposals to include foreign language study as a core skill in 16–19 education (National Curriculum Council, 1990a) are testimony to the importance now officially attached to the subject area.

It remains to be seen if the over-designed structures of the National Curriculum remain in place for long. The infelicity of its vocabulary and the arbitrary arrangement of some of its language content should not, however, distract us from realising that for the first time, the right to learn a language other than one's own is recognised in law. Kipling might have had other circumstances in mind when he wrote

'And what should they know of England who only England know?'

but the notion of a restricted experience is analogous to that received if the person has access to only one language. In the words of M. Byram (1992): 'This is particularly the case for speakers of English who fear no threat to their language even in a European community.' Because of the national and international dominance of English, the monoglot English speaker is at risk of not understanding the proper significance either of the multi-lingual nature of the British Isles or of the enormous linguistic variety of the rest of the world. Present expediency may emphasise the role of trade, but the fundamental importance of knowing something through experience of how people with another culture or ethnicity think and express themselves can only be of benefit in more fully understanding the realities of the world. That experience can only be unlocked through language skills.

It is in this sense that the reappraisal of the position of foreign language study in the UK curriculum can be welcomed as a major contribution to education for citizenship. By encountering and operating in another language, at however elementary a level, one is forced to reconsider one's view of the world and to grapple with the reality that the modes of expression which one takes for granted may only be arbitrary forms of conceptualisation shared by relatively few others. Elements such as language gender, verb inflection and adjectival placement, immediately perceived as different from that in English by learners of French, for example, or differences in script and relationships between sounds and written symbols, as met in non-European languages, serve to decentre the learner from the false security of assuming that the mother-tongue is the norm.

In a multi-cultural society such as that in the UK, this has a crucial role, as yet hardly exploited, in meeting the kinds of challenge set out by Lynch's articulation of goals for education in culturally diverse societies. His hypothesis emphasises the 'intercultural competence' and 'interdependence' (p.36) of groups of citizens in a multi-cultural society. (Lynch, 1992)

Recognition of the importance of language in aiding such competence is also part of the thrust of the movement among teachers of all languages towards developing Language Awareness programmes. (Hawkins, 1987;

James & Garrett, 1992). In such work, something of the nature of language is made explicit to learners, so that its significance in human society is highlighted. Language Awareness work can be encountered at all levels of education and embraces a wide variety of concepts. Languages teachers have a distinctive expertise to offer such programmes, which can draw from many curricular areas, and they have often been the leaders of Language Awareness developments in schools in which direct experience of operating in a number of languages is frequently linked with matters of more general linguistic import.

> The first-hand experience of another language brings a new perspective to pupils' perception of language, enabling them to make comparisons which sharpen their understanding of the concepts in both languages.
>
> (DES/Welsh Office, 1990).

This specifically linguistic aspect of the language learning experience has been cited as a major element of the subject's place in the National Curriculum, and further emphasises its role in providing an enhancement to citizenship education within the confines of our own national boundaries.

The kinds of learning activities widely recognised as good practice among effective languages teachers reflect a number of features enumerated in *Curriculum Guidance 8* (National Curriculum Council, 1990b), and relate to post-16 classes as well as those covered by the demands of the National Curriculum.

Thus the widespread use of pairs and groups in order to practise and develop oral work is a distinctive feature of languages classrooms. For this to be effective, learners have to listen to each other, negotiate roles and meanings, interact in a social context, give each other support and encouragement, and formulate conclusions often arrived at through negotiation and compromise. The content of such activities is frequently of a nature in which opinions are expressed because the learners are personally engaged, but it can, at an appropriate level of sophistication, deal with

> issues that have a wider import [about, for instance,] the world around us (e.g. town and country, land and sea, environmental issues, architecture and buildings) [or] the international world (e.g. travelling and staying abroad, national stereotypes, co-operation and conflict).
>
> (DES/Welsh Office, 1990)

It is a common feature of active language classes that learners are involved in collecting data (from authentic published material) or opinions (from surveys) to enable them to process conclusions on such issues.

The growth of the Graded Objectives movement forced the pace of introducing greater negotiation between learner and teacher in agreeing and setting targets and determining standards of performance. Ironically, in its early development, it was often only the learners who had been assigned to lower ability groups who had such an opportunity, and who thus became most adept at this skill.

The skills inherent in the use of IT are given a particular dimension in foreign language work. Clearly there are different conventions involved in producing accented or non-Roman scripts and a real purpose is present in learners' use of E-mail with partner institutions abroad. Properly prepared exchange visits with such partners give a tangible example of the Speaker's Commission's fourth element of citizenship education, 'the experience of the school as an institution playing a role in the wider community.' (quoted in Fogelman, 1991). If, as in most cases, the contacts and exchanges are with a school in Europe, the languages area is often the key to involvement in a wider European dimension (DES, 1992).

Language learning has an essential role in the education of future citizens, and is the unique key to full appreciation

> that they are citizens not only of the UK but also of Europe and the rest of the world. It encourages them to enter into and respect the attitudes and customs not only of other countries but also of the communities making up their own society.
>
> (DES/Welsh Office, 1990)

Fortunately the marginalisation of such an activity is no longer a danger, for language learning is now recognised as a right.

References

Byram, M. (1992) 'Foreign language learning for European Citizenship' *Language Learning Journal*, 6, 10–12.

DES (1992) *Policy Models: A Guide to developing and Implementing European Dimension Policies in LEAs, Schools and Colleges*. London: DES.

DES/Welsh Office (1990) *National Curriculum Modern Foreign Languages for Ages 11–16*. London:DES.

Dickson, P. and Lee, B. (1990) *Diversification of Languages in schools: the ESG Pilot project*. Slough: NFER.

Fogelman, K. (ed.) (1991) *Citizenship in Schools*. London: Fulton.

Hawkins, E.W. (1987) *Awareness of Language: An Introduction*. Cambridge: Cambridge University Press.

HMI (1977) *Modern Languages in Comprehensive Schools*. London: HMSO.

James, C. and Garrett, P. (1992) *Language Awareness in the Classroom*. Harlow: Longman.

Lynch, J. (1992) *Education for Citizenship in a Multi-Cultural Society*. London: Cassell.

National Curriculum Council (1990a) *Core Skills 16-19*. York: NCC.

Page, B. (1974) 'An alternative to 16+', *Modern Languages* , **55** (1), 1–5.

Page, B. and Hewett, D. (1987) *Languages Step by Step: Graded Objectives in the UK*. London: Centre for Information on Language Teaching and Research.

Van Ek, J. (1977) *The Threshold Level for Modern Language Learning in Schools*. Harlow: Longman.

70

ART

Martin Wenham

At first sight there might appear to be little connection between the individual imagination and creativity characteristic of art, and the collective responsibility, decision-making and empowerment which are the foundation of citizenship. Yet the division between them is more apparent than real, if only because many of the skills, attitudes and abilities which art education seeks to develop can contribute directly to decision-making and action in a public domain which has a profound effect on everyone: the quality of the visual environment.

As citizens, once we are outside our personal living space we inhabit a shared environment, with which we interact and which influences almost every aspect of our lives. Whether individuals are aware of it or not, both their actions and their attitudes are likely to be governed to a significant extent by the visual quality of their environment, whether it be pleasing and harmonious or ugly and strident; evidently well-maintained and cared for or broken-down and neglected. Collective decision-making and empowerment to conserve and improve the quality of the environment can be undertaken in an informed and rational way only if the present situation can be thoroughly understood, and the results of possible actions can be accurately predicted. But the ability to understand the visual environment and the ways in which it can be changed for the better depends on the development of more fundamental skills, such as visual perception, literacy and imagination.

Without the development of these basic skills, informed decision-making and action to conserve and improve quality in the visual environment are impossible. The present environment cannot be 'read' and analyzed into desirable, neutral or undesirable elements; nor can the interaction between these elements be understood. Without visual imagination developed through observation and experiment in a wide variety of media, the effect of changes in the visual environment can neither be predicted nor represented in a way which could inform collective decision-making and action. For example, *Education for Citizenship* (NCC, 1990f, p.25) suggests that pupils at Key Stage 3 could, as part of studying Democracy in Action, 'collect examples of local planning proposals (and) discuss reasons for the proposals and their likely impact on the environment and the quality of life'. The usefulness of any such discussion, in so far as it related to the quality of the visual environment, would be directly limited by the visual awareness and literacy of the pupils undertaking it.

Art Education and Visual Literacy

The most direct and obvious contribution of art to education for citizenship is in the development of visual awareness, literacy and imagination. Only relatively recently has it been widely acknowledged that art education to be fully effective cannot be confined to the ability to design and make. It must also include work explicitly aimed at developing the ability to see and evaluate critically one's own work and that of others. This awareness has been incorporated into the National Curriculum for Art (DES, 1992), in which both Attainment Targets are based on the growth of visual perception and literacy. AT 1 calls for 'The development of visual perception and the skills associated with investigating and making...' while AT 2 requires 'The development of visual literacy and knowledge and understanding of art, craft and design'. The overall aim of developing these abilities is summarized by criteria suggested in the Non-Statutory Guidance for Art (NCC, 1992, p.G2), that at Key Stage 3 'pupils should demonstrate that they can: analyse the appearance, structure and function of what they see and record their observations and ideas for different purposes; collect, analyse and organise relevant information to develop their own thinking, imagination and ideas'.

Art Education and Pupil Responsibility

Art Education has a second major contribution to make to education for citizenship, which may be less obvious but which is no less direct or important. This has its origin in the long tradition within art education of encouraging pupils to exercise choice and take responsibility for their own work. Recently, such 'active learning' has become prominent in thinking and policy-making for the whole curriculum (see, for example, Leicestershire LEA, 1992); but it has for many years been an essential feature of art education. The choice which pupils are encouraged and expected to exercise over the subject of their work and the materials and methods they use perhaps accounts for at least part of the popularity of art, especially at secondary level; but the attitudes of independence and responsibility it helps to develop are potentially of great importance to education for citizenship.

Art and Citizenship in the School Environment

The quality of the visual environment has a significant impact on the quality of life in all places which humans inhabit or visit; but particularly at Key Stages 1 and 2 the school environment is likely to be most important in education for citizenship (NCC, 1990f, pp. 10–11). This is because the school is not only the place where teachers and pupils interact most strongly, but also the environment over which they can co-operatively exercise the most control, and within which they can be empowered to take responsibility and bring about constructive changes.

Within the primary classroom, especially, the interaction between citizenship and art can develop strong foundations. Because children commonly feel a sense of ownership, that their classroom is their 'special place' within the school, they can the more easily be encouraged to assume collective responsibility for its quality as a visual environment. This involves 'reading' the familiar room critically, which in turn requires an arousal of visual awareness and a willingness both to observe afresh and to question the surroundings to which one has become accustomed. A critical visual reading of the familiar environment can form the basis for an *informed* discusion of good points, bad points and the need for change. It also makes possible the accurate prediction of the results of suggested actions and increased knowledge of the use of colour, texture, shape and form (among other, less visual factors) to bring about controlled change and improvement.

Such activities may be managed and directly related to the whole curriculum most readily in the primary school, but there is no reason why they should be confined to Key Stages 1 and 2. At any age, improvement of the classroom and school environment can be used as a focus for sharing decision-making, responsibility and achievement through perception, discussion and collective action, in which visual awareness and literacy have an essential part to play.

Art and Citizenship in the Wider Environment

Just as decisions, actions and learning within the classroom can be extended naturally to the school as a whole, work within the school relates to the quality of the wider visual environment which children experience. Ways of developing visual perception, awareness and literacy in the context of the built environment have been explored by Adams and Ward (1982), who point out (pp. 30–31) that

> The development of critical awareness is a desirable end in itself. But it is also vital if we are ever to have effective public participation in the making of decisions about the environment... Participation in discussion of the quality of the built environment depends, in the end, on the ability, first, to read the visual language of buildings and places and, second, to use the visual and verbal language of criticism. The more specific participation and political skills probably fall in subject areas outside the art studio, but art teachers have prime responsibility in the development of experiential, perceptual, analytical, critical and communicatory skills. Critical appraisal is for everyone.

The activities and programmes which Adams and Ward suggest, analyse and evaluate were developed originally for the 16–19 age groups and later for the whole secondary phase; but their principles and basic methods could equally well inform work with younger pupils. These principles were themselves derived from critical analyses such as those of townscape by Cullen (1961) and of landscape by Fairbrother (1970, 1974), which explore in depth the reading of the visual environment and the ways in which people respond to and interact with their surroundings. Such studies show very clearly the results of planning and development controlled (or not) by those lacking the visual skills, awareness and analytical abilities which can be developed only by art education.

There is, however, some reason to be cautiously optimistic. The requirement of the Art National Curriculum that visual perception and literacy should be systematically developed throughout the school age-range, coupled with the role of education for citizenship in developing 'the more specific participatory and political skills' to which Adams and Ward (1982, p. 31) refer, means that at least the framework for progress is in place. Whether the curriculum statement will be translated into curriculum as experience remains to be seen, but the potential for the abilities developed by art education coupled with the qualities of active, constructive citizenship can hardly be doubted.

The major cause of poor quality of visual environment is often said to be lack of investment and public funding. While more investment might remove limitations from particular projects which are worthwhile and which deserve more active support, the basic problem is a much deeper one. It is that too much of the environment, both urban and rural, is imposed on communities from without, rather than growing through changes originated and managed from within. This occurs largely by default. Even in the absence of deliberate malpractice and the withholding of information on the part of planning authorities (see, for example, Norman, 1972), citizens either do not know that they can, or do not feel competent to, make decisions for themselves or influence those of local government agencies.

Areas in which a high level of visual quality in the environment is consistently maintained are, almost invariably, inhabited by people who are both visually aware and whose skills of citizenship are highly developed. They assume collective responsibility for, and share in the maintenance of, the quality of their own surroundings. Preventing further deterioration, conserving what is desirable, eliminating the squalid, strident and ugly, as well as initiating positive new developments, are all activities which profoundly affect the lives of those who inhabit an environment, whether permanently as living space, or temporarily for work or leisure. This is the public domain in which art education and education for citizenship need to establish effective two-way communication, for without the perception of the artist the citizen is blind, and without the qualities of the citizen the artist is powerless. Together, they create the potential for significant and positive change.

References

Adams, E. and Ward, D. (1982) *Art and the Built Environment.* London: Longman.

Cullen, G. (1961) *Townscape.* London: Architectural Press.

DES (Department of Education and Science) (1992) *Art in the National Curriculum.* London: HMSO.

74

Fairbrother, N. (1970) *New Lives, New Landscapes*. London: Architectural Press.

Fairbrother, N. (1974) *The Nature of Landscape Design*. London: Architectural Press.

Leicestershire LEA (1992) *Leicestershire Curriculum Statement*. Glenfield, Leicester: Leicestershire County Council.

NCC (National Curriculum Council) (1992) *Art Non-Statutory Guidance*. York: National Curriculum Council.

Norman, D. (1972) *Public Participation and Planners' Blight*. London: Faber and Faber.

PHYSICAL EDUCATION AND CITIZENSHIP

Angela Wortley

Curriculum Guidance 8, while putting forward a plethora of ways and subject areas in which citizenship education can be delivered, does not include Physical Education in its suggestions. The Physical Education Non-Statutory Guidance document to support the teaching of Physical Education in the National Curriculum (NCC, 1992) has a corresponding lack of reference to suggestions for citizenship education. Both omissions seem glaring. Physical Education has long been perceived, rightly or wrongly, as a subject through which students experience challenging situations, develop courage, fitness and team spirit, recognise fair play, obey rules, etc. Society widely believes that physical education can influence the individual personality and help produce a better citizen. The value of outdoor education relies greatly on this notion and the perceived demise of competitive games in schools has been of national concern. Perhaps because of the extent of the overlap neither document felt the need to be more explicit!

In this chapter, areas within Physical Education lessons which can provide opportunities for citizenship education will be highlighted. In addition the potential for citizenship education within the whole area of Community/Physical Education partnerships will be examined. (Dance will be embraced within the term Physical Education throughout the chapter, as in the NCC 1992 document.)

Over the last decade classroom practice in Physical Education has been greatly influenced by curriculum development projects such as those producing the *Physical Education for Life* (Coventry LEA, 1984) document and the *Teaching and Learning Strategies in Physical Education* (BAALPE, 1989) report. These, when applied to the Physical Education National Curriculum document, will naturally provide opportunities for education for citizenship. The approaches to teaching, already widely adopted, in which students are enabled to take increasing responsibility for many aspects of their programme, ought to empower individuals to develop a personal statement about the value and place of physical activity in their adult lives, and to draw up a personal exercise plan.

Physical Education is the *only* curriculum subject in which students are given the opportunities to develop their physical capabilities to the full. As a basic need, exercise is essential for the normal development of the skeletal, muscular and cardiovascular systems of the body (Tanner, 1978). The beneficial effects of exercise are now well documented in the physical, social, psychological and emotional domains (Fentem, Bassey and Turnbull, 1988). In this context the experience of a full Physical Education curriculum is a basic right if individuals are to be given an opportunity to achieve their physical potential.

To enable pupils to achieve that physical potential and become know-
ledgeable practitioners, the Physical Education document stresses the
importance of the continuous process of *planning, performing* and *evaluating*. This illustrates the intention within Physical Education of developing
student independence. Indeed, within the general requirements for delivery
of the National Curriculum (NCC, 1992 p.3), those aspects relating to
developing independent learners and to developing positive attitudes coincide markedly with the objectives found in *Curriculum Guidance 8*.

Many of the objectives described in *Curriculum Guidance 8* can be
accomplished during Physical Education lessons.

– Most activities in the P.E. curriculum provide opportunities in which
  to experience the nature of *cooperation* and *competition*. Games are
  the obvious activity area for experiencing the real tensions of cooperation between team members whilst competing against others. The
  opportunities for cooperative learning occur continually in gymnastics, dance, outdoor activities, swimming, athletics and games.
  Cooperation is essential for *safe* practice in all these areas and for *any*
  practice in some, e.g. carrying and erecting heavy and awkward equipment in order just to take part.
– Opportunities to consider *fairness, justice* and *moral responsibility*
  occur frequently within lessons, in competitive situations outside
  lessons and in the world of sport. Although this is a controversial area
  there is a consensus of opinion as expressed by Parry (1986) that
  games can provide the opportunities for the presentation of values.
  More recent discussion in this area (Kirk and Tinning, 1990) suggests
  that Physical Education provides a key area in which cultural mores,
  values and symbols can be both produced and legitimated.
– Games, gymnastics, dance and outdoor activities provide opportunities for developing *problem solving skills*. The Games for
  Understanding approach developed by Thorpe, Bunker and Almond
  (1986) and now used widely, relies on those skills.
– The settings in which most Physical Education lessons take place provide opportunities for developing *personal and social skills*. These
  opportunities can be significantly enhanced by relinquishing to students some of the decisions about their curriculum. Students can be
  encouraged to make significant input into:
  (a) criteria for evaluation;
  (b) activity programmes;
  (c) extra-curricular activities;
  (d) school sports festivals;
  (e) team selection and training, drawing up fixtures, arranging trans-
      port, hosting visitors.
  Students could be given responsibility for negotiating and managing
  the budgets for activities where appropriate.

– Dance in particular can be used for exploring the different cultures and lifestyles that co-exist within our society. Inviting performing groups into the school can extend and enrich students' knowledge and appreciation of other cultures.

School and Community Partnerships

The *Physical Education Non Statutory Guidance* (NCC, 1992) includes a section entitled 'Partnerships, Physical Education and Sport'. The *Sport and Active Recreation Report* (DES, 1991) emphasises the importance of developing partnerships between many agencies. Of particular relevance to this contribution is the section on 'Young People and Sport' (pages 17–19). In the recent Sport Council's consultation document 'Young People and Sport' (1992) the role of developing partnerships to encourage and sustain participation is examined and many examples of successful projects are included. It is now widely recognised that a good school physical education programme will provide *only* the baseline in performance terms, but that a life time of involvement in sport and excellence can flourish from there. The reports referred to are testimony to the acceptance at the highest level that the production of elite performers is not a major objective of the physical education curriculum.

Therefore, if students are to develop their full physical potential the development of community links is vital. It will only be through such partnerships that physical education will be able to achieve a central aim of developing in individuals an active lifestyle, and education for citizenship ought to be a core element in that process. The partnerships will provide contexts in which students have the opportunities to experience the nature of community as recommended in *Curriculum Guidance 8*, and at the same time develop a knowledge and understanding of some of the complex relationships involved in issues relating to work employment and leisure.

The following are some opportunities for delivering education for citizenship.

– Providing students with the information about the sporting opportunities that are available to them and, importantly, how they can participate – for example, by joining a club or leisure facility, booking facilities and joining classes, finding out about coaching opportunities.
– Encouraging students to organise festivals and events for themselves, other schools and the community – sporting celebrations are an important part of our cultural heritage.
– Exploring the responsibilities of performers and audiences at sporting events and how their actions can affect the community both positively and adversely.
– Providing opportunities through partnership to experience 'how provision for leisure relies on local and national government, private enterprise and voluntary effort' (NCC, 1990f p.9).

– Developing links to enable students to help in the organisation and administration of sport; creating routes for becoming competent or qualified officials through national and local sports organisations.

Curricular developments suggested in the Coventry LEA document, *Physical Education for Life* (1984), and further developed by Almond (1989), include more examples of how citizenship education can be an integral part of physical education. These writings predated the recent rebirth of the term citizenship and describe these examples under other headings (such as learning to compete, sharing in learning, ownership of learning, interpersonal competences, personal development, leisure studies and learning away from school).

How effectively citizenship education can be delivered through physical education will depend on the time allocated and the importance attached to it throughout all key stages. Too little time will deny students the ability properly to exercise their rights. They will have gained insufficient knowledge from their experiences to participate fully, exercise knowledgeably or contribute positively to the sporting life of the community.

References

Almond, L. (1989) *The Place of Physical Education in Schools*. London: Kogan Page.

BAALPE (1989) *Teaching and Learning Strategies in Physical Education*. The British Association of Advisers and Lecturers in Physical Education.

Coventry LEA (1984) *Physical Education for Life: A framework for developing the Physical Education Curriculum*. Coventry Local Education Authority.

DES (1991) *Sport and Active Recreation*. London: Department of Education and Science.

Fentem, P.H., Bassey, E.J. and Turnbull, N.B. (1988) *The New Case for Exercise*. The Health Education Authority and the Sports Council.

Kirk, D. and Tinning, R. (1990) *Physical Education, Curriculum and Culture: Critical Issues in the Contemporary Crisis*. London: Falmer Press.

NCC (1992) *Physical Education in the National Curriculum*. York: National Curriculum Council.

Parry, J (1986) 'Values in Physical Education' in Tomlinson, P. and Quinton, M. (eds.) *Values Across the Curriculum*. London: Falmer Press.

Sports Council (1992) *Young People and Sport: A Consultative Document*. The Sports Council.

Tanner, J.M. (1978) *Education and Physical Growth*. London: Hodder and Stoughton.

Thorpe, R., Bunker, D. and Almond, L. (1986) *Rethinking Games Teaching*. Department of Physical Education and Sports Science, University of Technology, Loughborough.

MUSIC

Linda Hargreaves

Education for citizenship is concerned with participation, cooperation and competition, and the development of the social skills, values and attitudes which contribute to these. It requires children to know their rights and responsibilities as citizens of a democratic society, and to respect those of others. Its major content areas include the nature of community, the pluralist society, the family, and work and leisure. I shall try to show that music in schools already takes in many of these objectives, and that there are numerous areas of overlap between the National Curriculum documents for music (DES, 1992) and citizenship education.

Music and community

Music has always been an important link between school and community through concerts and shows. Plummeridge (1991) describes the social processes integral to both music and citizenship which are evident when children take part in a public performance:

> the artistic excitement and social cohesion that is generated [when] pupils of different ages, abilities and backgrounds are working together in a cooperative manner and sharing a common commitment to the success of the venture. This involves being conscious of their responsibility within a team and recognizing and respecting the contribution of the others. (p 116).

In addition, rehearsals for these occasions demand 'an enterprising and persistent approach to tasks and challenges' i.e. demonstration of an attitude which education for citizenship seeks to develop.

From performance to participation

The traditional performance role for music must be extended further, however, to move towards 'establishing the importance of positive *participative* citizenship'. Music in the National Curriculum requires children to plan and carry out performances for different audiences, with different purposes and in a variety of contexts. These tasks provide a genuine context for some of the examples of activities such as looking for similarities between their own favourite songs and those their parents listened to when young, or finding out what music is enjoyed by different sections of the community. They will be exploring, simultaneously, the citizenship components of family and community, and, when given responsibility for organising a performance, practising the study skills of 'examining, selecting and rejecting resources', and 'planning, organising, completing...tasks' (NCC, 1990f).

Citizenship through music implies going beyond performance, however, to making music together. Here are some examples of how this has been done:

- family choirs for parents and children to sing together;
- a percussion workshop for visitors and children to play together as part of a primary school Open Day;
- secondary students invited shoppers to 'have a go' at playing electronic keyboards set up in the shopping arcade as part of the town's Arts Week;
- a joint 'school and community arts committee' to plan the community arts programme.

Examples like these show how different generations and groups can work together, and have the potential to reduce prejudice, increase mutual respect and lead to school-community partnership.

Citizenship embedded in musical activities

Evidence of the objectives of citizenship embedded *within* musical activities such as composing and performing is shown in a teacher's report on an invention project carried out by a class of six year olds.

- *Communication skills: arguing a case clearly and concisely* . After listening to several pieces of recorded music, the children were asked to say what they thought of when listening to each one. 'By the last piece of music they were able to verbalise their ideas confidently.'
- *Attitudes: respect for different ...opinions and ideas* . They composed their own music in small groups and 'listened carefully to each others' attempts...were positive in their comments... made suggestions about how they felt improvements could be made'.
- *Values: examine evidence and opinions and form conclusions.* On listening to a tape of their work, 'They decided that they should all play all of the time.' They tried this, but then realised that 'they could not hear each group – 'it's just a noise!' was one child's comment.'
- *Being a citizen: the balance between individual freedom and social constraint.* They decided to 'overlap' each section but this proved difficult. One child said, 'It's better when we watch our leaders and just play when they do.' (J. English – unpublished work for University of Leicester, Certificate in Professional Studies in Education (Music) assignment).

This account shows that 'reception teachers can work mightily for cooperative citizenship' (Lynch, 1992), whilst Bean and Oldfield (1991) offer a plethora of simple music activities, which specifically target social skills such as waiting a turn, exchanging things, being the centre of attention, and listening to others.

Classroom climate and citizenship

Successful education for citizenship depends on classroom climate (Lynch, 1992). In the example above, the teacher's strategies stressed cooperation, trust, and pupil ownership of their work. These aspects of classroom climate are not easy to achieve, however, and teachers have to discipline themselves to watch, listen, wait, but not intervene (Galton and Williamson, 1992). Secondary teachers must be able to adopt this style when necessary where peer group influence is very strong, and students may be reluctant to express original or dissenting views (see Dynneson and Gross, 1985).

Disembedding citizenship skills

How can the processes embedded in musical activities be disembedded and applied to social contexts? Firstly, the children need to know what skills they have used, perhaps by analysing a video of a group working, and, secondly, in a democratic classroom climate, they need to use them, and reflect on their use, in other contexts, such as:

- debating their rights and responsibilities in school as regards music-making and noise pollution.
- simulating an 'Arts committee meeting' trying to decide whether to sponsor (i) a tour by a wind ensemble of students from a Russian state; (ii) a group of Asian musicians to work in a school; or (iii) a charity concert by a local rock group.
- discussing the responsibilities of rock stars as role models for young people.

Music in a pluralist society

The Citizenship guidance document refers directly to music only in relation to the pluralist society, recognising the many different cultures within our society. Music in the National Curriculum concentrates largely on the Western symphonic tradition, however. Many teachers lack confidence about using non-European music and this provides a genuine reason to give children more responsibility and to learn from them. This might arise naturally in a multi-ethnic school, from the research into family preferences mentioned above. Music educators offer conflicting advice here: Swanwick (1988) advocates the use of a wide range of musical styles, whereas Walker (1990) suggests extensive work with 'culture-free' sounds, to reduce children's dependence on Western musical values, before embarking on in-depth study of one non-Western music. Mills (1991) proposes that children themselves join this debate, giving teachers the chance to hear their opinions and respond to stereotyped and negative attitudes. Indeed, since children are the citizens of the school community, perhaps they have a right to participate in the debate about the content of their educational lives.

82

References

Bean, J. and Oldfield, A. (1991) *Pied Piper: Musical activities to develop basic skills.* Cambridge: Cambridge University Press.

DES (Department of Education and Science) (1992) *Music in the National Curriculum.* London: HMSO.

Dynneson, T. and Gross, R (1985) 'An eclectic approach to citizenship: developmental stages' *The Social Studies* **76**(1), 23–7.

Galton, M. and Williamson, J. (1992) *Groupwork in the Primary Classroom.* London: Routledge.

Gulbenkian Report (1982) *The Arts in Schools.* London: Calouste Gulbenkian Foundation.

Lynch, J. (1992) *Education for Citizenship in a Multicultural Society.* London: Cassell.

Mills, J. (1991) *Music in the Primary School.* Cambridge: Cambridge University Press.

Plummeridge, C. (1991) *Music Education in Theory and Practice.* London: The Falmer Press.

Swanwick, K. (1988) *Music, Mind and Education.* London: Routledge.

Walker, R. (1990) *Musical Beliefs: Psychoacoustic, Mythical and Educational Perspectives.* New York: Teachers College Press.

RELIGIOUS EDUCATION

Mark Lofthouse

'Religious education is dead, long live citizenship'. This partly humorous, partly fearful comment was scribbled by an R.E. teacher at the end of an in-service course, where she had been studying the connections between religious education, moral education and citizenship. The comment forcefully articulates the anxiety felt by many R.E. specialists that their curriculum area is now the subject of a take-over bid; the 'God slot' without God, religious studies without religion – in a word, citizenship.

Before such fears can be dismissed as over-reaction, some underlying issues need to be teased out because they directly contribute to the fears felt by R.E. teachers. The National Curriculum Council's *Curriculum Guidance 8: Education for Citizenship* has been described as an imperialist document, in the sense that it annexes territories and lays claim to spheres of influence, which have traditionally fallen within the religious education and social science domains. In his article, 'Citizenship, diversity and education', Terry McLaughlin (1992) explores some of the visible tension inherent within *Curriculum Guidance 8.*   He argues that the document contains both minimal and maximal interpretations of the concept of citizenship (pp. 235–250). The end product of a maximal interpretation is the morally autonomous citizen of the world, unlikely to disturb most teachers, since the utopian vision, if ever to be realised, would envelop and dominate every part of the curriculum. The minimalist position, however, is far more likely to arouse the subject sensibilities of R.E. specialists. By arguing for the virtues of voluntary activity, linked to basic social morality, advocates of a minimalist interpretation of citizenship (McLaughlin p.241) open the way for religious education to become a secularized contributor to personal and social education (Ford, 1992). While it could be argued that this is a logical outcome of the secular drift of British society, it should be emphasized that McLaughlin is not advocating it. On the contrary he argues strongly for a maximal interpretation of citizenship, where rights as well as duties, are explicit (McLaughlin p.253).

This stance should offer intellectual assurance to R.E. teachers that their distinctive concerns are not forgotten. Yet even more relevant to them is the precision with which philosophers such as McLaughlin and J. and P. White (J. White 1990, 1992 and P. White, 1991) demolish the interchangeability of language deployed by government ministers. Seizing upon the new inspection framework for schools, McLaughlin ponders how newly appointed inspectors are to judge the spiritual, moral, social and cultural development of pupils in schools. Additionally, he questions how inspectors are to assess the responses made by pupils to opportunities presented to them to 'exercise responsibility, community and citizenship' (McLaughlin p.252). Behind the babble of words there is a profound silence.

The problem is one of imprecision. It would seem that ministers and politicians of all persuasions have read *Alice in Wonderland*. They all appear to believe that words mean exactly what they wish them to mean. Hence the underlying insecurity of R.E. teachers, who, in the last decade, have seen religious knowledge equated with personal and social education, transmuted by moral education and finally subsumed into something called citizenship.

In facing up to such intellectual incoherence, R.E. teachers should resolutely deny themselves the luxury of simply giving in. Instead they should exercise a tough minded realism, which may save both their sanity and their subject. Religious education is ultimately concerned with spiritual issues and questions. As a subject it confronts students with the possibility of a God (or some kind of divine presence), active in the world and not to be relegated to the sidelines of cultural history. In considering these seminal issues, it can be deduced that religious education is essentially concerned with exploring beliefs and values and how these determine decisions and behaviour.

Having established this, R.E. teachers should be quite confident about the uniqueness of their subject contribution, since other curriculum areas then drop naturally into place. All important behaviours involve decision making through reference to a belief system. Beliefs often, though not universally, include belief in a deity or some kind of spiritual reference point. Decision making is about right and wrong, and thus religious education is certainly about moral education. It is also about citizenship, because the latter can be argued to be about beliefs, morals, values and right and wrong (McLaughlin's maximal interpretation). At its best, therefore, citizenship can be classified as religious education and moral education in action.

Viewed in this light, the fear expressed by the teacher in the opening quotation is premature – religious education and citizenship can be natural allies. However, the alliance needs nurturing. The palpable distress and unhappiness of R.E. teachers stems in part from the story of Everybody, Somebody and Nobody. Everybody is supposed to be attending to the spiritual, moral, social and cultural development of pupils as demonstrated in their responses to community and citizenship. Somebody (a name in the senior management team?) is meant to be coordinating policy and practice, while Nobody (the R.E. teacher, if there is one?) is, for the most part, uncertain what the words mean in terms of action. In the face of such confusions and uncertainties, compounded by shortage of staff and curriculum time, many schools fall back to implicit models hinted at in *Curriculum Guidance 8*. Ethos and team approaches are relied on to fill in the values gap. Senior managers claim that ethical dimensions are covered by the humanities team. A community aspect, it is argued, is embedded in assemblies and charitable events. In short, everything is in place but what is in place is intangible, unclear and imprecise.

R.E. specialists might feel much happier if they were properly assertive in challenging the vagaries of implicit models. If they need fresh ammunition, the 1992 White Paper, *Choice and Diversity: A New Framework for Schools* (HMSO, 1992), is studded with references asserting the importance of religious education and its role in promoting values and citizenship models within schools and their communities (e.g. the section on 'Schools and a Moral Dimension (p. 7), and on 'Voluntary Schools' (p.32)). The White Paper offers a rationale for R.E. teachers to involve themselves in the task of curriculum mapping, a means by which implicit models can be replaced by guidelines, demonstrating where and when ethical questions are being addressed across the National Curriculum. R.E. teachers should play a key role in this activity and should not be afraid of using citizenship as a means of establishing curriculum coherence. On a recent in-service course, for example, teachers found the question of where laws come from and how they are applied, a particularly fruitful way of bringing together R.E., moral education and citizenship.

In such a co-operative context it is easy to recognize that R.E. and citizenship need each other. Kelly (1988) is one of many writers scathing in his condemnation of the utilitarian nature of the National Curriculum. A partnership of R.E. and citizenship studies affords the opportunity to rescue the National Curriculum from the poverty of what Kelly sees as its unstated ideology. The unique role for religious education and R.E. teachers is to infuse concepts of citizenship with possibilities of the divine. It is urgent that R.E. teachers forcefully argue the case. A failure to do so could leave both citizenship studies and the National Curriculum in a secular slough of despond.

References

Ford, A. (1992) 'Personal and Social Education: a new competitor for the R.E. slot in schools,' *Church Times*, 2nd October, p.10.

H.M.S.O. (1992) *Choice and Diversity: A New Framework for Schools*. London: HMSO.

Kelly, A.V. (1988) *Damage Limitation: The Challenge of the Education Reform Bill.* University of Liverpool, Department of Education Occasional Paper, May 6th, 1–33.

Mclaughlin, T.H. (1992) 'Citizenship, diversity and education: A philosophical perspective,' *Journal of Moral Education*, 21 (**3**).

White, J. (1990) *Education and the Good Life, Beyond the National Curriculum*. London: Kogan Page.

White, J. (1992) 'Can education for democratic citizenship rest on socialist foundations?' *Journal of Philosophy of Education*, **26** (1), 19–27.

White, P. (1991) 'Humanisation, democracy and trust: The democratisation of the school ethos', *Studies in Philosophy and Education*, **11** (1), 11–16.

CHAPTER 6

Other Contributors to Education for Citizenship

EUROPEAN AWARENESS

Max Buczynski

Curriculum Guidance 8 suggests eight essential components for the content of education for Citizenship. The first is the broad area 'the nature of community'. One 'community' which is increasingly important for everyone today, especially young people, is the European Community. It is in this context, and with an awareness of the wider objective of the whole curriculum that 'Education should and must develop pupils' potential to the full and prepare them for the world in which they live' (*Curriculum Guidance 8* p.1), that European Awareness (EA) should be considered.

In February 1986 the twelve member states of the European Community signed the Single European Act which came into force in July 1987. The Act set a target date of 31 December 1992 for the completion of what is commonly referred to as the 'Internal Market'. Therefore whilst '1992' has nothing to do directly with education, the free movement of people, goods and ideas will have a considerable effect on an educational system which is expected to prepare young people for adult life in which Europe will be a reality.

In January 1988 the DES funded the 'European Awareness Project' administered by the Central Bureau for Educational Visits and Exchanges. It included twelve pilot LEAs. The report on the European Awareness Pilot Project suggests that to define it as a 'precise objective or a generally understood destination which enables people to assert "Ah now I have it! Now we have arrived!"' should be resisted; it is seen 'more as a clutch of attitudes, skills and experiences concerned with diminishing ignorance and lessening misunderstandings' (DES, 1990 p.8).

The LEA working groups focus on the curriculum from 5 to 16 but note that there are important initiatives for VI Forms, and students in Further Education and Higher Education. Indeed the Northamptonshire E.A. Project set up in 1989/90 is aimed at post-16 students in VI Forms and Further Education and the basis of the model used by them, piloted at Prince William School, will be explained later. The LEA working groups also included the youth service, adult and community education and special schools.

Having discussed and found possible locations for EA, the LEA working groups considered the question 'How is E.A. delivered?' They found that a considerable range of discrete subjects can contribute to the development of EA. They include modern foreign languages, history, geography, music, science, economics, business studies and vocational courses. Not surprisingly, the LEA working groups emphasised the importance of a cross-curricular approach as a particularly effective means of delivery.

It would appear that there is no subject or area of the curriculum which cannot contribute to the development of EA. Indeed, speaking at the Centre for European Education conference in November 1990, Edith Pagliacci, Professional Officer of the NCC, linked the European Dimension to the implications of the Single European Act as well as to the policy objective agreed in 1989 by the twelve member states. This established the desirability of: a multi-cultural Europe; a mobile Europe; training for all in Europe; a skilled/competent Europe; and an open Europe to be achieved by 1993. The NCC (Edith Pagliacci said) particularly linked the European Dimension to the cross-curricular theme of citizenship. It sees the way forward for preparing citizens of Europe as through 'more links; a broad and balanced curriculum for all; more languages; and a curriculum which recognises the UK's membership of the EC.' The National Curriculum will provide a basic entitlement to EA as it includes the study of a modern foreign language to the age of 16, but to ensure EA for all there is a need to link the objectives of EA to the delivery of the National Curriculum more widely.

EA is clearly linked to attainment targets in Geography, History (particularly in Key Stage 3) and Modern Languages (where it is important that it should offer insights into the culture of other countries to encourage mutual understanding). However, these are not exclusive and any subject can be orientated to make a contribution. For example, in English at Key Stage 1 clear opportunities for delivery of EA are offered by: using stories from different cultural sources; reading signs, labels and notices; and using information sources.

The NCC has outlined five cross-curricular themes and EA should permeate these. For this to happen careful planning is essential. In the absence of specific fuller guidance from NCC schools will find great difficulty in achieving cross-curricular provision, but this must be their aim.

At the same European education conference in November 1990, Kate Seager, a Professional Officer from SEAC, explained how examining groups will be required to demonstrate how they have taken account of the

European Dimension. From 1994 it must be embedded in all GCSEs. At 'A' Level all examining boards will have to show how their syllabuses from 1994 share the principle of 'awareness of the European Dimension'.

The project at Prince William school in Northamptonshire has been established to create a programme of European industrial, economic, political and cultural awareness for VI Form students. The partners in the pilot project were the school, British Steel plc, and the Koninklijk Atheneum II (KAII), a 14–18 school in Gent, Belgium. Funding for the pilot project was made available by the Central Bureau and the LEA (Central Bureau for Educational Visits and Exchanges 1991).

At Prince William, there is a thriving programme of language exchanges, but many students are still leaving school without experiencing the benefits of an exchange visit. It was decided that a group of seventeen economic/business studies students would be an ideal cohort for the pilot project which took place in February 1990.

There are five strands of awareness that we wanted to develop through the project:

- *Industrial* – students to be aware of the range and diversity of industries in Europe, from multi-nationals to small firms.
- *Economic* – students to appreciate that the economy in which many firms are now operating is increasingly European rather than National.
- *Political* – students to develop an understanding of the decision-making processes: the European Parliament, the Commission and the Council of Ministers.
- *Cultural* – mistrust and prejudice are too often based on ignorance. Understanding other people and societies is of educational and, ultimately, economic value.
- *Residential* – to live with a foreign family is a unique opportunity to learn something of the life-style and values of a different culture.

We chose Belgium for a number of reasons. The country is prosperous and Belgians enjoy a high standard of living. Brussels is officially a bi-lingual city, is home to several European institutions, and is the de-facto capital of Europe. Most young Flemings learn English, and as with other groups whose mother tongue is spoken by few, the motivation to succeed is high. However, because the teaching of Dutch is almost non-existent in British Schools, Flemish Schools find it virtually impossible to organise exchanges with the UK.

Lastly, Belgium is physically close and has good communication links with the UK, thus making travel easy and cheap. The initial contact with the Koninklijk Atheneum II was made by the Central Bureau's Schools Unit. On the return visit Belgian students spent seven days at Prince William School, experiencing British family life and above all speaking English, their main objective.

On the exchange, Prince William students in Belgium were expected to keep a diary of visits which would be used in writing a project. As a result of the success of the pilot project, the Humanities Department, with teachers of History, Geography and Communications at 'A' level, expressed a strong interest in participating in an extension of the project. Exploratory discussions have also been held with a view to incorporating the project in the Experience of Work/Enterprise module of the Four Counties Modular General Studies 'A' Level Syllabus.

One of the conclusions of the European Awareness Project was that one 'of the most effective ways of developing European Awareness is by providing pupils with first hand experience of a foreign culture', and, similarly 'opportunities for travel, work and study abroad must be made available to the widest range of pupils, students and teachers'. In particular they specify 'vacation jobs, work experience, environmental partnership links, exchange visits and study visits' as giving young people opportunities for 'participation, co-operation, problem solving and decision making' (DES, 1990 p.13).

A recent development has been a course available from the A.E.B. for 16–19 years olds, the Certificate in Contemporary European Studies. From September 1993 Prince William School will be offering this one year course. The course has been designed for delivering the European Dimension. It involves schools making links with at least one other institution in the European Community through the use of electronic mail. The course develops an understanding of European issues, skills in information technology, comprehension of a different understanding of industrial and economic matters and the ability to present ideas and information in an interesting way.

In conclusion it can be seen that, with a flexible approach to interpreting and implementing the NC, creative teachers can use the European Community as a resource. This will allow students to explore and discover the Community for the mutual benefit of all.

References

Central Bureau for Educational Visits and Exchanges (1991) *European Awareness, Report No.1: Development Projects 1989/9.* London: Central Bureau for Educational Visits and Exchanges.

DES (1990) *European Awareness Pilot Project: June 1988–Jan 1990.* London: Central Bureau for Educational Visits and Exchanges.

POLITICAL EDUCATION

Frank Conley

The relationship between citizenship and political education is ambivalent. From one point of view they are the same thing: for example Alan Howarth, speaking to the Politics Association in 1990 implied this by saying that 'through the foundation subjects, political education will become the experience of the many rather than the privilege of the few.' On the other hand *Curriculum Guidance 8* does not mention political education at all, preferring to refer vaguely to social sciences.

The truth, as usual, lies somewhere in between. The citizen's obligations to the wider needs of the community make citizenship wider than political activity, but an understanding of politics is essential in realising Duncan Graham's assertion that citizenship 'helps (pupils)... to understand the duties, responsibilities and rights of every citizen and promotes concern for the values by which a civilised society is identified – justice, democracy, respect for the rule of law' (*Curriculum Guidance 8*, Foreword).

The first task of schools is 'helping pupils to acquire and understand essential information' (*Curriculum Guidance 8*, Foreword). Understanding politics is a vital part of this process. In their policy statement '*Citizenship: the Association's Position*', the Politics Association (1990) identifies a substantial body of political knowledge proper to Citizenship. As well as the fundamental institutions of our political system such as Parliament, central and local government and the electoral system, this includes rights, duties and concepts.

There is ample evidence that this knowledge can be readily conveyed and understood by pupils of all ages. The Hansard Society's Mock Election in the spring of 1992 showed the enthusiasm with which primary and secondary school pupils can respond to political processes. The selection of candidates, the organisation of meetings and the process of election attracted attention throughout the British Isles, and provided a valuable basis for the development of citizenship. The Autumn Visits Programme organised by the House of Commons Education Service is regularly over-subscribed, and even younger children respond with enthusiasm to learning about the workings of Parliament in the building itself. Children can respond equally readily to concepts if clearly explained and related to their own experience. Even primary-age children can appreciate concepts of authority, power and representation, and every parent knows how rapidly the concept of 'fairness' is grasped.

The conveying of knowledge is comparatively straightforward and uncontroversial, and few teachers of politics would disagree with Alan Howarth's belief that 'political education at school which presents fairly the diversity of opinion in our society but is firm on the resolution of differences through our democratic institutions and the courts of law best serves the interests of young people' (see above, 1990). The question of attitudes is more difficult. In their policy statement the Politics Association urges 'recognition of the importance of freedom, toleration and fairness; respect for the truth and for reasoned argument…[and] the desire and the confidence to take an active part in the democratic political life of their community and nation'. For school students 'community' must of necessity include 'school', and *Curriculum Guidance 8* recognises as much when it states that the second task of schools is to lay the foundations of citizenship by providing pupils with 'opportunities and incentives to participate in *all aspects of school life*' (my italics). It is not the purpose of this chapter to suggest ways in which schools can be organised to provide pupils with opportunities and incentives for active participation. Whether schools are managed 'democratically' or not, there are major issues where political education can provide significant help.

The first problem is the attitudes of pupils. A school, as Jim Cordell (1992) says of a liberal democracy 'works best when disagreement about details is dealt with against a background of agreement about fundamentals'. Adolescents are bound to concentrate on the first aspect and ignore or be unaware of the second. They are understandably concerned with what affects them directly, and likely to be hostile to actions by authority which they regard as unreasonable. Thus discussions of schools as models of political communities tend to become purely anecdotal about specific issues such as uniform, with teachers in the unenviable position of having to defend decisions with which they may not be in sympathy. Yet there can be great value in using the school to explain the wider workings of politics by relating it to pupils' direct experience. Such differing concepts as authority, power and the rule of law can be suitably exemplified particularly if the school is one of a number of institutions cited in this way, along with the family, clubs, societies and other organisations.

Much also depends on the attitudes of teachers. One of the most important problems raised by political education is bias. Opponents, particularly from the Right, argue that teaching politics is bound to be slanted, so that pupils are being force-fed with the teachers' own distorted values. It is unfortunately true that nothing can be done about *deliberate* bias, nor is this necessarily confined to the Left, but as Bernard Crick has written (1987) 'more students switch off when they hear the rising whine of the preacher's voice than are moved to action, still less thought'. It is not true, either, that anything can be taught in a *totally* objective, value-free way. To quote Crick again, such an assumption 'contains, assumes or conceals a doctrine'.

The important thing, as politics teachers have known for years, is not to avoid bias but to identify it and to handle it in a thorough and professional way: the former is the more difficult, but once achieved it makes the latter easier. There is a substantial body of literature discussed by Bernard Jones (in Conley, 1991 p.11), including an especially significant article by Alex Porter (1986) which deals analytically with the ways in which biased messages can be conveyed or opportunities for alternative points of view denied. Much of this may come as a surprise to teachers who are unaware how greatly students can be influenced by style and body-language as much as by actual words. This applies to teachers' attitudes to discussion of 'school politics' as considered above, as much as to more overtly political questions.

The effective handling of accusations of bias is part of the process of increasing confidence among teachers in handling political issues. Such issues are controversial, which may lead teachers to avoid them unless they are sure they know what they are doing. There has been a serious lack of encouragement or support from official circles for all the cross-curricular themes, and no guidance as to what teachers should actually do in the classroom. Now that the theory is largely in place the next stage must be to provide practical materials, and for these there is already a basis in the books produced for teaching politics at GCSE and before: a practical contribution of politics teaching to citizenship education.

The final set of attitudes to consider belongs to the management of schools. As well as overcoming the problem of governmental indifference or disapproval, headteachers, governors and parents need to be reassured about citizenship in many ways. It takes courage for a head to agree that there should be discussion of decisions rather than automatic acceptance, and the disciplines of politics teaching can help to show that questioning can be constructive rather than subversive, especially if it is part of a whole school policy. Governors and parents are in an increasingly political and powerful position which makes them suspicious of indoctrination. It is essential that they should know that a school has a fully-devised programme for citizenship based on clear principles of balance (see Smith, Southworth and Wilson, 1985). Such programmes already exist where politics is studied as a GCSE or A-level subject: now politics teachers and all supporters of citizenship must ensure that non-examined programmes become equally acceptable.

I make no apology for devoting more space to attitudes than to knowledge in discussing the relationship between citizenship and political education. Conveying knowledge is relatively easy: attitudes and 'action skills' cause much greater problems, but are much more important. H.D. Lasswell (1948) defined education as the passing on of accepted skills. The skills of political education are essential to the teaching of citizenship, and can also ensure that they become fully accepted.

References

Conley, F. (ed.) (1991) *Political Understanding across the Curriculum*. London: Politics Association.

Cordell, J. (1992) *Essential Government and Politics*. London: Collins.

Crick, B. and T. (1987) *What is Politics?* London: Edwin Arnold.

Lasswell, H.D. (1948) *The Analysis of Political Behaviour: An Empirical Approach*. London: Kegan Paul.

Politics Association (1990) *Citizenship: the Association's Position*. London: Politics Association.

Porter, A. (1986) 'Political bias and political education' in *Teaching Politics*, September. London: The Politics Association.

Smith, J., Southworth, M. and Wilson, A. (1985) *A Course in Political Education for 14–18 year olds*. London: Longman.

PERSONAL FINANCIAL MANAGEMENT

Ian Duffell

I have been a bank manager for many years, in large branches and in small, and my experience has taught me that as far as money is concerned most people don't really understand the subject at all. Where this applies, in common with people who find it difficult to read or write, individuals become adept at hiding the fact. Many people seem to take the first mortgage or life policy that is offered to them, whether out of fear or ignorance, when other arrangements could leave them much better off by retirement.

Only a small proportion of families have any sort of written budget, month by month or week by week. This must mean that holidays and other commitments are booked and entered into with a vague feeling that 'it will all sort itself out.' No wonder 2.5 million families in the UK currently face serious debt problems according to the Policy Studies Institute (Berthoud and Kempson, 1992).

Before anyone stereotypes me as an uncaring banker let me say that many people find themselves in financial difficulties through no fault of their own. At one end of the scale, in 1992 the Maxwell pensioners had no chance of protecting their investments against fraud. The same could be said regarding some customers in 1990 banking with BCCI which was closed owing to massive fraud by the senior management (although for some years City wags had joked that the initials stood for the 'Bank for Crooks and Criminals International'). Unemployment, especially during the recession, is often not the fault of the person concerned and this can often lead to financial problems. One step up the scale are other investors who lost money through fraud, which they could not have predicted, but who chose to invest in a high risk/high return organisation ignoring the aspect of high risk (e.g Barlow Clowes in 1989).

Many people in the UK did not expect mortgage interest rates to rise so far, nor house prices to fall so much over the last few years, yet the possibility was always there. I well remember discussing with numerous customers in 1988 that house prices could not carry on rising as they had done and that they could actually fall. This was generally disbelieved. Some people however are authors of their own misfortune by recklessly applying for several dozen personal loans or credit cards, ignoring advice to compare APRs and/or ensuring that they can meet repayments. Some articles in the press recently have complained that credit is too easily available yet many people used to complain when mortgages and credit were difficult to obtain. (Who remembers mortgage queues?) In a free society wise individuals exercise the self-restraint not to be greedy with credit facilities just as they do not leave sweet shops with dozens of Mars bars.

Who is to teach this self-restraint, this simple skill of comparing APRs or the more difficult skill of choosing the best mortgage? Previous generations were not perhaps so tempted with credit because there were fewer financial services and the majority of people dealt only with cash. Their choice was more limited but if wealthier parents had a bank account they tended to introduce their children to the same branch once they were old enough. Most people avoided debt and saved via 'The Man from the Pru' or his equivalent on doorsteps.

With the explosion of financial services in the 70s when the banks went 'down market' many young people, without appropriate parental guidance, acquired cheque books and credit cards and learnt by trial and error. This was possibly much the same as when motor cars became popular – initially no driving test was required. However, when the number of accidents reached unacceptable proportions the need to prove proficiency became evident and the driving test was introduced. Society benefited although personal freedom was marginally curtailed.

No one would now argue against teaching road safety to children or campaign for the freedom to drive without having passed a test. The number of hours necessary to learn to drive (say 10–20) is probably the same needed to teach someone the basics of personal money management. Once the fear of the concept has been eradicated many people could go on to read financial pages out of genuine interest or at least shop around for the best deal on a mortgage, life policy or pension plan with confidence just as they might for a new bedroom suite.

I do not know of any other mechanism for teaching all young people other than via the schools. Many schools do accept that part of a 'broad and balanced education' (Education Reform Act, 1988) in the 20th Century must include some lessons on budgeting and financial planning. However, some teachers fight shy of this topic giving reasons such as 'There is no room in the timetable' or 'We do not feel qualified to teach this subject in depth.' Others feel it is up to the Banks to teach this topic, which is not really very practical as they have little contact with schoolchildren and would probably be accused of marketing to minors if they did.

The concept of citizenship involves the relationship between the individual and the community. Without reasonable health, and the availability of adequate services it could be argued that the individual cannot exercise the fundamental rights of citizenship. I believe that citizenship is underpinned by several fundamentals including that of personal money management. No one can function as a full citizen if their financial worries keep them awake at night and their daylight hours are spent avoiding creditors or worrying about bailiffs.

Schools could do much to enhance the future quality of life of their pupils in this area. Whatever the income of the individual, budgeting is advantageous. Bear in mind that many pupils will have over £1 million pass through their hands by the time they retire. Teachers can make a difference regarding how much is lost or frittered away and how much is spent or invested wisely.

I would suggest that useful areas to cover would be:

> budgeting; sensible use of credit; interest on loans and savings and APRs; leaving home; working and paying tax; college and grants; mortgages; investment; handling debt problems.

I would like to encourage discussion in staff rooms and at governors', or parents' meetings, to see if a whole school policy for teaching about money can be developed. Numerous styles can be considered (see CSCS Broadsheet No 35, Citizenship and the Art of Handling Money) and if the will exists money management can be introduced in a cross-curricular way so that all departments have a chance of using their specialism, whether this be in Maths or English, Geography or History, RE or Drama. It may be in some schools that a core course such as PSE or tutorial time may be an appropriate place for a module on money. All schools could develop a spiral of learning so that the children receive a non-conflicting message of the importance of handling money properly.

Many teenagers have part time jobs and an easy way of catching their interest is to compare rates of pay, hours and conditions. This can lead on to lessons regarding budgeting and planning for major purchases such as CD players. Many sixth formers will be aiming at higher education and a chance to see the grant application form, student insurance forms, tenancy agreements and so on in advance will give them confidence that they can handle these matters when the time comes.

Primary school children are not too young to start their spiral of learning and there are examples of projects with 5/6 year olds running a shop in school to improve their mental arithmetic (four apples at 20p each) and the change necessary at the till when a £5 note is presented. Others have been shown the video 'The Curious History of Money' (free hire from Barclay's 0733 67622. See also CSCS 1992) which amusingly covers barter and the development of coins. Yet others have visited the Bank of England Museum/Exhibition where the youngsters are interested to see a million pound note and some real gold bars.

Many resources are available to help teachers prepare lessons – I have come across over 100. Many are free and I would encourage any Citizenship Co-ordinator to collect several packs, selecting from them appropriately to form a planned series of lessons for different age groups. Different teachers can mould the pack to their requirements – sometimes only a third of the resource is used but new videos and books are coming out every few months so it is worth enquiring of local banks and building societies as well as educational publishers.

Some schools invite local bank managers in, either to talk about money generally, or to conduct role plays in front of a class so they know what to expect when they apply to open an account, ask for an overdraft or get into financial difficulties. There are some schools which resist such visits but I feel they are very relevant and empowering for the young people. Research some years ago by the Inter Bank Research Organisation showed that many people preferred to visit their dentist than their bank manager. Hopefully that is changing. Banks are trying to be less intimidating and more user friendly. Interestingly, the 'intimidating' aspects (imposing entrances, stone columns and marble floors) are a hangover from the public fear of the last century that Banks could go bust, so everything was aimed at giving the impression of a solid institution. Nowadays bank failures are so rare that the preferred style is a domestic 'lounge' with carpets and a sofa.

Most pupils will spend many hours of their lives working for money – you could help them learn how to make it work for them via the intelligent use of savings and loans. An aversion to credit is not the answer as few people could afford a house without a mortgage. Similarly, carefully planned credit for major purchases such as cars or a new kitchen can be life enhancing for the individual and job creating for society. (A large reduction of consumer credit could add 1 million to the unemployment figures.) Deprivation is often expressed in economic terms; if your pupils could become financially literate you might lead them to take control of their lives rather than letting them be victims of ignorance.

References

Berthoud, R. and Kempson, E. (1992) *Credit and Debt: The PSI Report*. London:PSI.

CSCS (1992) *Broadsheet 35: Citizenship and the Art of Handling Money*. Northampton: Centre for the Study of Comprehensive Schools.

COMMUNITY

Chris Jones

Throughout the evolution of community education since the days of Henry Morris in the 1930s (see Ree, 1984) three broad currents have merged which Martin (1987) describes in detail. Despite the differences there are a number of key principles which are most commonly shared. Among these are:

- social, political and economic needs should be addressed holistically with education as one element in the organic whole;
- community education sees the teacher more as facilitator thereby introducing equality and self-determination into learning;
- learning is lifelong and occurs in formal and informal settings.

In *Education for Citizenship*, the National Curriculum guidance document, the curriculum components represent either points of delivery for community education or aspects of the social, political and economic life of communities it serves. Community educators aim to improve social cohesion whilst celebrating diversity, for example. The family is recognised as a potent learning institution, public services are partners in inter-agency approaches.

Where there is the greatest resonance is in the underlying ethics. It is clear from the National Curriculum document that education for citizenship cannot be delivered without due attention to attitudes and values and the twin approaches of participation and partnership. In putting the document into practice, teachers will have to acknowledge that pupils are already members of the community, that their diversity must be valued, that the School is only one player and that pupils must go beyond its gates in the course of learning, that pupils need the skills as well as the knowledge to be participating members of their community.

In order to illustrate these ideas the remainder of this chapter describes a project entitled 'Citizenship through the Community' which was carried out collaboratively by CEDC and the Centre for Citizenship Studies in Education.

It is not surprising that the Community Education Development Centre and the Centre for Citizenship Studies should enjoy a productive partnership in a collaborative project. The two organisations are founded on many similar educational principles, making us natural allies.

The project's key characteristics were:

- methodology would focus on pupil participation and self-directed learning;
- equality of opportunity would always be a prime consideration;
- community representatives would be involved in a partnership throughout all stages of curriculum development.

Four schools that agreed with these principles and had a proven record of innovation joined the project in September 1991. They were: Victoria Junior School and Rushden Secondary School in Northamptonshire and Wallbrook Primary School and Coseley Secondary School in Dudley. One teacher from each school, together with a number of community representatives, met for two days during the autumn of 1991 to plan for the implementation phase, the bulk of which took place in the winter term of 1992. The project was viewed not as an end in itself but as a launch into citizenship and especially into a closer relationship with the schools' local communities. It was for this reason that all the schools agreed that pupils at their various levels of ability would engage in local research. They were to find out who was in their community, which organisations – social, economic, political – operated there, how it had changed in the past, what it would be like in the future and who would be the prime movers in that change. All agreed that pupils should be encouraged to see the potential for making change rather than see themselves as passive victims of it. This was an exceptionally ambitious brief which proved especially taxing for those teachers operating on their own rather than as members of a team.

During the project four main issues exercised teachers. Details of research sometimes buried the issues of citizenship, so keeping hold of the concepts became important. Building a sustainable partnership was another as were the models of implementation chosen by the schools. Perhaps the greatest issue was managing the learning process. With such a wide brief and a commitment to self-directed learning, it became imperative that teachers devised checks and controls on how pupils worked and what they were learning. Guidance for other teachers on handling these issues and a sample of activities are included in Jones, 1993.

Here I will focus on two issues – partnership and controversy – which arose during the project and may be of interest to readers intending to engage in similar work. To illustrate the first I will recount a tale told to me by the manager of a volunteer bureau who became involved in our project. A school in her area arranged for all their pupils to collect their discarded toys in the run-up before Christmas. These were then to be donated to poor, deprived children. The headteacher contacted the volunteer bureau to ask if some poor children could be found so that the press could photograph them receiving their gifts. Happily, the manager declined the request but sadly there was no real opportunity for dialogue. Had there been, I suspect that the pupils might have been involved in very different activities, ones more likely to engender finer values.

Teachers often talk of partnerships. Frequently what they mean is that they have planned a piece of curriculum development, crossed the t's and dotted the i's and then drafted in someone for a particular purpose. There is nothing wrong with this approach except that it is not a partnerhsip. It is not even a consultation. The draftee is more a kind of three dimensional visual aid. A partnership implies equality, a common purpose and a shared ownership. For this both must work together from the start. The prospect of this worries teachers, fearful that roles will become blurred or that they will be vulnerable – curriculum planning can be a messy business and some are afraid to wash their dirty linen in public.

Such fears are usually unfounded. The distinction between teacher and partner is quite clear. The teacher is the expert in the managment of learning, the partner brings a specific expertise to that learning. The hurly burly of curriculum planning meetings – of deciding anticipated learning outcomes, of choosing methodology, of negotiating time, resources, space, of persuading reluctant colleagues – firmly locks the partner into the whole project. The project design is enriched by the new, 'outside' perspective and the partner becomes fully committed, hooked. The skill and dedication of teachers working under adverse constraints of time and resources usually inspires considerable respect from their new partners.

Such a partnership can bring a friend for life and prove a valuable source of support. One teacher in the project had insufficient interest and support from colleagues. As a consequence the partnership became increasingly important. On several occasions I witnessed the partner offering moral support and practical help.

Teachers came to our first planning meeting with one or two initial ideas to develop. Interestingly, they all involved pupils doing 'something nice' for residents at old people's homes. In discussion we decided it was for two reasons. Teachers had not had the opportunity to think about citizenship in any depth and tended to think no further than 'good' citizenship. Secondly, it appeared a safe, uncontroversial option. It was ironic then that in pursuing a commitment to self-directed learning a visit to an old people's home was the catalyst to the most controversial work done in the project.

On their visits, the pupils were alarmed to find the residents in some considerable distress because they had just heard that their home was to be closed and they were moving elsewhere. Upset by this, one child wrote to the local newspaper which, to his astonishment, printed his letter. Encouraged by his success, other pupils followed suit, writing also to the Director of Social Services, who, besieged by complaints at this unpopular decision, complained to the education authority that pupils were being used for political ends. What teachers had seen as an unexpected bonus in learning outcomes soon soured as complaints rippled through the corridors of the education authority. Fortunately, this teacher's worst nightmare scenario was transformed into very positive outcomes.

All the pupils involved were given a simulation in which they had to decide which two of three community resources would be closed and which one would remain open. The group representing the social services committee was helped by the Director of Social Services who, to his credit, responded to our request. He worked very well with the pupils and was amazed by the sophistication of their thinking. 'We can't close the nursery because parents will have to give up their jobs and then they'll be expensive to keep on social security' as an observation from a nine year old, was indeed impressive!

There were two lessons for us. First, the community, even the peaceful backwaters of an old people's home, harbours all manner of conflicts and tensions. Second, that pupils given control over their own learning may well unleash controversy in unplanned ways. In this case, the headteacher faced the issue with considerable aplomb and had the project coordinator as an additional and external support. A less experienced teacher, operating with little support, could have come adrift.

Just two aspects of the project have been highlighted here, but the project proved a rich seam of ideas which CEDC would like to develop in future. In particular, we hope to build on linked work where some pupils have been engaged in community enterprises and where other have become involved in local issues. Taking the two issues of change and participation we are particularly keen to pursue projects which put young people in the driving seat to improve the quality of life in their neighbourhood. This project has paved the way for such developments.

References

Jones, C. (1993) *Citizenship Through the Community: a handbook for teachers.* Warwick: CEDC.

Ree, H. (ed.) (1984) *The Henry Morris Collection.* Cambridge: Cambridge University Press.

Martin, I. 1987 'Community Education: towards a theoretical analysis' in Allen, G., Bastiani, J., Martin, I., and Richards, K. (eds) *Community Education: An Agenda for Educational Reform.* Milton Keynes: OU Press.

There are several 1992 publications from CEDC relevant to Community Enterprise in the curriculum. Full details of these and other materials can be found in the Resources Catalogue, CEDC, Lyng Hall, Blackberry Lane, Coventry, CV2 3JS. Tel: 0203 638660.

DRAMA AND THE TEACHING OF CITIZENSHIP

Neil Kitson

At its simplest, drama is a story which is enacted either for ourselves or for a group of others. In content it is a metaphor of reality (Bolton, 1986). It is not reality nor should it pretend to be reality. What it does is to mirror or portray 'real life'.

> Playing a role which involves either simulation or second-handedness should not be confused with a genuine commitment to role.
>
> Peters (1981 p.77)

Through working in this fictional way we are able to gain insights into ourselves and others. It is a form of action through which learning takes place not just through our participation but more significantly through the discussion and reflection upon the events that occurred within the drama. Drama carries with it a variety of labels such as 'role play' and 'simulation' but what is common to all is that they use a fictional form in which there is a problem to overcome or a challenge to be met and these are coupled with a degree of tension.

Drama is an activity which draws upon a form of behaviour that has its roots in early childhood play. Through play we are able to learn about ourselves (Rogers, 1954) and through playing someone else we can aid our personal development. Drama is a very natural and accessible form of learning for young children and older students alike. It is most effective where the teacher provides a supportive learning climate which can accommodate exploration and experimentation – luxuries not usually afforded in real life.

What are the general advantages to both the pupils and teachers of working in this way? These are by their nature inter-related and can be summarised as follows.

The drama process:

- provides a meaningful context in which to see and convey the significance of abstract information;
- allows the teacher a structure through which to encourage the pupils to explore beneath the obvious;
- allows pupils to test out and explore a range of attitudes, ideas and issues;
- creates situations where pupils can see the consequences of their actions and decisions;
- enables individuals to test out ideas which can be drawn upon in the future;
- offers safety and protection from failure, as any decision can be changed and re-enacted to obtain a different outcome, thus enabling the teacher to create an infinite number of opportunities for learning;
- generates motivation for learning both within drama and subsequently

in other curriculum areas;
- allows individuals to bring their concerns to the drama situation either directly or in role;
- lets us see the world from ihe view point of others;
- is a collaborative and co-operative group process.

What is the relationship between drama and citizenship?

The main purpose of drama is the exploration of personal dilemma and social interaction, of attitudes and of morality through a fictional form and it does this by being a shared and co-operative activity. It takes as its contexts (and through its process uses) those elements of education that have been brought under the umbrella of citizenship. The opportunities that drama offers can therefore accurately reflect the fundamental aims of citizenship:

> – to establish the importance of a positive participation in citizenship and provide motivation to join in – to help pupils to acquire and understand essential information on which to base the development of their skills, values and attitudes towards citizenship.
> *Curriculum Guidance 8* p.2

Drama then, is able to take one fictional example of an issue or concern and give it a sense of reality. It offers the teaching of citizenship a context for learning and can help develop altruism and empathy (Hoffman, 1970). It can take the abstract notions set out in the citizenship curriculum guidance, such as the family or public services, and through story use the fiction as a metaphor which can be examined and discussed. To illustrate this more fully what follows is a range of examples that show how drama can give access to the requirements set out in *Curriculum Guidance 8* for knowledge, skills, attitudes, moral codes and values.

Knowledge

The nature of community.

- How communities are organised and the importance of rules and laws.
Key stage 1. The children are in role as people ship-wrecked on an island. They must decide how to organise the food and shelter and what the rules should be.

- How communities reconcile the needs of individuals and those of society.
Key stage 2. In the role of designers and town planners pupils attempt to put forward plans for a new shopping centre. They are then confronted by the teacher in the role of a representative of the town's wheel-chair population.

Roles and relationships in a democratic society.

- Similarities and differences between individuals and groups and communities – diversity and interdependence.

Key stage 3. As a group of economists and scientists the pupils attempt to persuade a farmer in the Amazon region not to cut down his trees, only to find that he wants the money to buy a jeep and jeans like theirs.

• The experience and opportunities of people in different roles and countries. Key stage 4. In the role of refugees from Sarajevo the pupils try to establish what they must do to rebuild their lives.

Cross-curricular Skills

Communication Skills

• Detecting opinion, bias and omission in evidence.
Key stage 4. In the role of journalists the pupils set out to discredit a sports star whom they have just found out has taken performance-enhancing drugs. They must decide who to interview and what to write.

Problem solving skills

• Recognising and defining the nature of a problem.
Key stage 2. The children, in the role of staff at a school, sort out a case of bullying, drawing upon the evidence from teachers, parents and children.

Personal and social skills

• Working with others.
Key stage 1. As the helpers at the zoo we arrive one morning to find that there has been a heavy fall of snow in the night. Many of the animals are in danger. What should we do?

Attitudes

• Respect for different ways of life, beliefs, opinions and ideas.
Key stage 2. As a group of Aztecs we are banned from praying to our gods. How do we protest?

Moral codes and values

The majority of drama work is based upon the notions of moral dilemmas, values and beliefs. By encouraging the children to work in this way they are being offered the opportunity to:

- compare values and beliefs held by themselves and others and identify common ground;
- examine evidence and opinions and form conclusions;
- discuss differences and resolve conflict;
- discuss and consider solutions to moral dilemmas, personal and social;

- appreciate that distinguishing between right and wrong is not always straightforward;
- appreciate that the individual's values, beliefs and moral codes change over time.

Drama offers teachers a unique method of teaching citizenship which engages the pupils and motivates them. Teachers who work in this way find that they are able to challenge, stimulate and create a wide range of learning areas. It is not suggested that drama be the sole method of teaching citizenship education but due to its effectiveness it should be part

> of a balanced range of teaching methods that support the active involvement of pupils in lessons.

> (NCC, 1990f, p.10)

References

Bolton, G. (1986) *Selected Writings on Drama in Education.* London:Longman.

Goffman, E. (1974) *Frame Analysis.* Middlesex: Penguin.

Hoffman, M.L. (1970) 'Moral development' in Mussen, P.A. (Ed.) *Carmichael's Manual of Child Psychology.* New York: Wiley.

Peters, R.S. (1981) *Moral Development and Moral Education.* London:Unwin

Rogers, C.R. (1954) 'Toward a theory of creativity', *A Review of General Semantics,* **11**, 249–60.

SOCIAL SCIENCES

Tony Lawson

While *Curriculum Guidance 8* suggests that citizenship education can be delivered in a variety of contexts – through the teaching of the subjects of the National Curriculum or other time-tabled provision, or through participation in the life of the school generally – a closer examination of the knowledge, skills and attitudes with which citizenship is concerned, reveals a concentration on areas and activities which have traditionally been the province of the Social Sciences. Politics is clearly aligned with the main ideas behind citizenship, but Economics and Sociology also have a considerable overlap with the content and skills suggested in the Curriculum Guidance document.

In terms of the eight essential components identified, the sections on Community, the Family, Democracy and Work, Employment and Leisure are areas which have traditionally been the concern of A level Sociology (AEB, 1992). Economics is also well represented in the sections on Work, Employment and Leisure, as well as Public Services. Moreover, when these components are broken down into descriptions of areas that should be covered, the text is littered with concepts which have usually been delivered through Social Science courses. For example, social stability and social change have been central concepts in Sociology GCSE syllabuses (SEG, 1991), while wealth creation and taxation are traditional areas in the study of Economics.

Similarly, in examining the cross-curricular skills put forward in *Curriculum Guidance 8*, there is an obvious overlap with the skills developed by traditional Social Science courses, such as 'detecting opinion, bias and omission in evidence', or 'interpreting statistics'. Even in those areas which are less susceptible to assessment procedures, such as Attitudes, or Moral Codes and Values, there is a similarity between the overall aims of Social Science syllabuses and the Guidance Document's lists such as 'examine evidence and opinions and form conclusions'. The match between education for citizenship and Social Science courses is not, of course, total. Yet there is sufficient similarity to suggest that education for citizenship could best be delivered through some form of Social Science provision. This is unlikely to be the case, however.

In terms of Key Stages 1 and 2, there is no mention of the Social Sciences as having a distinctive input to the teaching of citizenship themes. Only at Key Stages 3 and 4 is there explicit mention of the Social Sciences and Economics, and only then tacked onto the end of lists of Core and Foundation subjects of the National Curriculum. Clearly, the Social Sciences are seen as additional subjects through which citizenship may be delivered. But given the pressure on the time-table because of the National Curriculum and other demands which may be made on student time, the

Social Sciences cannot be seen as a necessary context for the delivery of material which has traditionally been their concern. Many schools, either through choice or staffing constraints will not be offering Social Sciences at Key Stages 3 and 4 and there will therefore be no guarantee of a Social Scientific input into the teaching of citizenship. For example, in the national survey of citizenship carried out by Fogelman, only 28 per cent of schools mentioned Economics and 28 per cent cited Social Studies as areas within which citizenship topics were delivered (Fogelman, 1990 p.87).

While this may seem to be an unintended consequence of the demands of the National Curriculum, there is a school of thought which suggests that there is a deliberate attempt to marginalise and exclude the Social Sciences from any positive influence on the curriculum in general and citizenship studies in particular. The Government's intentions in re-activating the concept of citizenship have been the subject of much speculation. Motives suggested have ranged from the desire to save money (Rankin, 1989 pp.28–29) to a political attack on the notion of social citizenship which has dominated since World War 2 (Foster and Kelly, 1990 p.73). However, Chris Brown has argued that the way citizenship is construed is to prevent the emergence of Social Science based citizenship courses (Brown, 1991). Government hostility to the Social Sciences stems from a conception of Sociology in particular as a left-wing discipline, inimical to the operation of a modern capitalist economy (Marsland, 1987). The Government has therefore, it is argued, 'used the concept of citizenship within the National Curriculum to redefine the traditional Social Sciences and marginalise their input to the periphery of the curriculum by lumping them all in the cross-curricular themes' (Singer, 1992).

But the argument can be taken further when the definition of citizenship favoured by the Guidance Document is considered. By focusing on the Active Citizen, the Government has rejected the more collectivist view of the post-war welfare state consensus and the more libertarian view of the New Right. However, the Government has also moved away from a definition of citizenship which is associated with the rights of being a citizen, to one in which the emphasis is placed on duties. As Rankin has pointed out, the active citizen is one whose acquisition of wealth is legitimate as long as the duty to contribute to society is also accepted (Rankin, 1989 pp.18–23). This results in a definition of citizenship which is hard to disagree with, but one in which the emphasis is on duty and obligation rather than citizens' rights and social justice.

This can be seen clearly in the suggested activities for the various Key Stages of the National Curriculum. The emphasis here is on the contribution to the community which Citizens can make through their voluntary activity, from running the school shop at Key Stage 2 to organising fun runs at Key Stage 4. Moreover, there is a central role in these activities for a whole range of official and semi-official bodies, from the police, whose contribution is ' of the greatest importance', to voluntary and religious organisations. But this is to present one aspect of citizenship as the only legitimate way in which citizenship studies should be developed and presents an official view of the functioning of society as the natural way of looking at the world. As Davies asks, 'Where is the notion of the protection and expression of human rights in civil and political, social and economic, and cultural context? Where is the willingness of the state to ensure that rights as well as obligations and duties are guaranteed?' (Davies, 1990/91). As Brown reported, some Heads rejected *Curriculum Guidance 8* as 'prescriptive, conservative and value-laden' (Brown, 1991).

But citizenship need not be like this. Indeed, as Marquand (1989) argues, the concept is a double-edged sword, because if young people are taught to think independently as a 'preparation for citizenship in adult life' (NCC, 1990f p.1), then they may come to realise that the role, as defined by the Guidance Document, is all duties and no rights. It is the lack of a critical edge which is the most serious flaw in the Curriculum Guidance Document. If citizens are to be active citizens, then young people need to engage in the sort of critical thinking which can lead them to transformative action in society, and which has been the traditional hall-mark of Social Science subjects in schools. This lack of critical focus, it could be argued, comes about precisely because citizenship has been divorced from the Social Scientific context, which can provide the knowledge and rigour necessary for a serious engagement by students in the consideration of the rights and duties of a citizen.

It is the involvement of Social Scientists in citizenship courses which can prevent them from ending up as old-style Civics courses or the encouragement of 'good works'. Social Scientists have training and experience in presenting controversial issues in a balanced and logical way. They have the knowledge base and interest to ensure that students are informed about their rights and duties as citizens. The alternative to a strong Social Science input into curriculum planning for citizenship may be delivery in a peripheral way by teachers who are uncomfortable and potentially biased with the material they are asked to present.

Therefore, rather than a marginalisation of the Social Sciences, the introduction of citizenship studies should be seen as an opportunity for Social Science teachers to establish themselves firmly in the pre-16 curriculum. If they can contribute effectively to the knowledge base and skills associated with citizenship wherever it appears on the curriculum, they can establish a solid foundation for students to continue studying the Social Sciences post-16, and in the process, might just prevent citizenship ending up as Religious Studies without the religion.

References

AEB (1992) *Sociology Advanced Level Syllabus*. Guildford: Associated Examining Group.

Brown, C. (1991) 'Continuities in Education for Citizenship', *Social Science Teacher*, **20**(3).

Davies, I. (1990/91) 'Are you an active citizen?', *Talking Politics*, **3**(2).

Fogelman, K. (1990) 'Citizenship in our Secondary Schools', *Social Science Teacher*, **19**(3).

Foster, S. and Kelly, R. (1990/91) 'Citizenship: perspectives and contradictions', *Talking Politics*, **3**(2).

Marquand, D. (1989) 'Subversive language of citizenship', *Guardian* 2.1.89.

Marsland, D. (1987) *Bias Against Business: anti-capitalist inclinations in modern sociology*. Harrow: Educational Research Trust.

Rankin, M (1989) *Active Citizenship: Myth or Reality?*. Berkhamsted: Volunteer Centre UK

SEG (1991) *GCSE Sociology Syllabus*. Guildford: Southern Examining Group.

Singer, J. (1992) *The Place of Citizenship in the National Curriculum*. Unpublished Paper, available from the author, School of Education, Leicester University.

COMMUNITY SERVICE AND VOLUNTEERING

John Potter

Citizenship is about each of us having a personal stake in the community. Knowledge of rights, responsibilities, law and history is necessary; but the experience of taking part and making the world a better place is central. Schools are charged by the 1988 Education Reform Act to 'prepare pupils for the responsibilities and experiences of adult life'. This challenge can only be met by every school having a clear grasp of how community service and volunteering are central to the effective education of the whole person. Community service and volunteering are not the icing on the education cake, something to decorate the curriculum if time remains once the demands of core and foundation subjects have been met. They are at the heart of effective, life-long learning. They are also the touchstone of a school's involvement with its local community.

There are two issues: first, the urgent need to enlist the help of local volunteers to support students in their studies and, secondly, the complementary need for students to experience the opportunity to enrich the life of the school and local community as a regular part of their studies.

Community Volunteers: Improving Performance

All schools are committed to ensuring that their students succeed to the best of their ability. The harsh fact is, however, that between 1987 – 1990 an average of 9 per cent of pupils in England left school with no graded examination results. In inner London the figure was 21 per cent. Furthermore, only '20 per cent of 16 year olds start A level courses and at the end of two years a third of them fail and have nothing to show for it.' (Sir Bryan Nicholson, quoted in *The Guardian*, 14 July 1992). There are Cassandras who are quick to produce even gloomier – but often more contentious – statistics. The most disadvantaged young people are those who grow up in a climate where little is expected of them and insufficient personal help and encouragement is given them at the moment when they most need it. Our present education system favours middle class pupils actively supported by adults who recognise the value of education. 'A minority is being trained for leadership and active citizenship, while the less advantaged majority become consumers and followers' (Roberts, 1991).

Educators in the public, private and voluntary sectors are increasingly realising the value of systematically inviting adult volunteers into school to work alongside teachers in supporting students in their formal studies and other activities. At CSV Education we are actively involved – through our Learning Together programme – in enabling college students to volunteer as tutors in secondary and primary and schools throughout the UK. Over ninety institutions of Higher and Further Education are currently (autumn

1992) involved in local student tutoring schemes that benefit all concerned and fresh schemes are coming on stream every month. The volunteers usually go into school once a week to work for one or two terms with a given group of pupils. The evidence is that all parties benefit significantly from these initiatives.

Employees from local firms are increasingly volunteering to help in school. In London's King's Cross, CSV has arranged for volunteers from a bank, an engineering firm and from CSV head office to work in a local multi-cultural primary school. The head teacher of Winton school strongly supports the scheme and points out that 'adult contact in inner city schools gives the children another dimension and provides a lot of fun'. Alan Bugg, an employee from Travers Morgan commented, 'It's giving me the opportunity to mix with children – something I haven't done for fifteen years. By working with the children for thirty minutes twice a week, I can rekindle my youth and come away feeling totally refreshed as well as gain important friends.' The reactions of the student tutors are equally positive. More traditionally, of course, parents and retired volunteers are equally a powerful resource for ensuring that pupils enjoy the support, skill and encouragement that they need to succeed in their studies. Nationwide, CSV is involving 1600 retired people in volunteering, of whom 300 are going regularly into schools.

Student Volunteers Enrich the Community

'The voluntary acceptance of responsibility for the well being of others is the hallmark of democracy,' said Lady Margaret Simey speaking of her work with the voluntary movement in Liverpool (1991). The habit of contributing creatively to the well being of the community cannot be learnt too young. CSV encourages pupils and students in full time education to learn that habit as a part of the taught – and whole-school curriculum. The future of volunteering in the United Kingdom will depend significantly on the extent to which young people are given the opportunity, confidence and encouragement to play their part in the life of their school and wider community.

Beaupre Primary School near Wisbech has built vital links with a nearby sheltered home for elderly people. Activities include residents from the home supervising school children with craft activities and the construction of a Queen's 40th Anniversary Garden, which is shared by the residential home, Beaupre Hall, and the school. Part of the wall separating the school from the home has been knocked down and an attractive gateway built to link the school and the Hall. 'The new gate is symbolic of our forging new links in the community', says headteacher, Steven Hales, when describing the achievement to visitors.

North London is now home to a growing number of refugee Turkish and Kurdish children. Some of them have lost their parents and live alone in bedsits. Sixth form students at George Orwell school have set up a voluntary language club run in the lunch hour. The work focuses on a variety of games, all of which have a sizeable language content. For example, the Sixth formers play scrabble with tutees, insisting at all times on the correct spelling of the words and checking in conversation that the boys understand the meaning of the words. They are also prepared to offer pupils help with homework or a piece of classwork.

New Approaches to Volunteering

These fresh and challenging approaches to volunteering are based on the simple premise that everyone – pupils, students workers, local and retired people – can volunteer. The evidence is that the great majority – once *asked* to help – respond creatively and with a real sense of pleasure. Such an approach demands that schools, colleges, workplaces and local groups break out of the mould that once kept them isolated from one another like the residents of Beaupre Hall before the wall came down.

'Schools are no longer isolated learning monasteries,' points out Leslie Silverlock, previously of Somerset Local Education Authority. 'They have become vibrant centres of local life. Without their local communities they would also find it very difficult to deliver the National Curriculum.' (CSV, 1992a). He has worked with CSV to create a set of practical case studies based on work in ten Somerset schools demonstrating how the vision of active citizenship can be integrated within the practical and technical demands of the National Curriculum.

Warwickshire LEA has worked with CSV on creating an in-service training manual for teachers who plan to deliver active citizenship within the curriculum. The examples are all based on practical experience in real schools (CSV, 1992b).

Community service – like patriotism – is not enough. Effective citizens are those who can make good things happen. Properly applied, the enterprise skills of problem solving, motivation, teamwork and communication are the lifeblood of democracy. CSV and others are promoting community enterprise in universities and schools. Coventry University, for example, has pioneered community enterprise as an option for students in all faculties. In more and more schools throughout the country community enterprise and action is a stimulus to the 'voluntary acceptance of personal responsibility for the well being of others' for which Margaret Simey calls. She then adds, 'It is essential for the survival of our way of life that the right to love our neighbours, freely and without compulsion, wins recognition as the true basis of all citizenship' (Simey, 1991).

References

CSV (1992a) *Your Community in the National Curriculum: Somerset LEA*. London: Community Service Volunteers.

CSV (1992b) *Developing Citizenship – INSET pack: Warwickshire LEA*. London: Community Service Volunteers

Roberts, K. (1991) 'Young Citizens', *Social Science Teacher* **20** (2).

Simey, M. (1991) *Active Citizens: New Voices and Values*. London: Bedford Square Press, p.108.

INTERNATIONAL CITIZENSHIP

Patricia Rogers

> Schools all over the world should pay more attention to international problems so
> that young people will see more clearly the dangers they are facing, their own
> responsibilities and the opportunities of co-operation – globally and regionally as
> well as within their own neighbourhoods.
>
> (The Brandt Report, 1980).

Citizenship

A citizen is a full member of a community. The acknowledgement that all
people should have full citizenship rights was enshrined in the Universal
Declaration of Human Rights (UN, 1985). The elements of citizenship can
be summarised under three categories: social, political and civil (Speaker's
Commission, 1990). Each element involves rights and responsibilities –
rights for ourselves and responsibilities for each other.

To be effective citizens, we need not only to be aware of our own rights
and the structures that exist to support them; we also have to be active in
ensuring that our fellow citizens enjoy their rights. We need to be aware of
how these rights can be undermined and of how to strengthen them.

The International Dimension

Citizenship involves membership of a community. The concept makes
sense for members of any group whose actions and decisions affect each
other. These include family, school, religious or interest group,
nation/state, the EC, the Commonwealth, and the largest of all, whose identity as an interdependent community is often stressed by calling it 'the
global village'.

Each citizen of the world has social rights that include: basic health care;
shelter; clothing; food; clean water; a safe environment; and education.
However, many people do not actually experience these fundamental
necessities of life. More than one billion people (about a fifth of the world's
population) live on less than a dollar a day (World Development Movement,
1991). More than 35,000 children die each day (UNICEF, 1992). Many,
also, do not have adequate civil rights – such as freedom of belief or speech
– nor adequate political rights – such as in electing their governments.

The structures and means through which we can exercise our responsibility to ensure the full rights of citizenship for all include: the United
Nations and its agencies; our own governments – local and national; voluntary organisations; and many aspects of our lifestyles – such as our
involvement with commercial companies, our behaviour as tourists and our
uses of resources. We can work through all these structures and means –
through voting, direct personal contacts, lobbying, fund-raising, support of

active voluntary groups, shopping, being considerate, and other forms of personal involvement.

Education for World Citizenship – Theory

What is needed

Being an effective citizen needs particular attitudes, knowledge, understanding, skills and experience. Developing these is a lifelong, evolutionary process – like education. It is also like education in that a basic foundation is best established while a person is growing up.

To develop the attitudes and patterns of behaviour of responsible world citizenship, schools need them to permeate the whole curriculum from the very start of schooling. Global citizenship education is not something that can be taught in occasional, isolated periods, nor is it something that can be started later, when other habits and attitudes have been established. Much of the specific information future effective world citizens need to acquire will be learned in particular subjects – but the attitudes and many of the skills need to cross subject boundaries. It is impossible to separate out a school's aspirations for its pupils' personal, social and academic achievements from its implicit model of citizenship. By making this model explicit, greater consistency can be achieved.

In 1976, the UK was signatory to the Paris Recommendation which pledged educational time for the pursuit of international understanding, peace and co-operation. In 1977, the then Department of Education and Science published a consultative document, stressing the importance of a strong international dimension in the curriculum because, 'we live in a complex, interdependent world and many of our problems in Britain require international solutions' (DES, 1977).

There is scope for focus on these dimensions in all the National Curriculum subjects and cross-curricular themes. CEWC (1992) shows this in some detail as it analyses the English and Welsh National Curriculum by subject and theme. It emphasises, too, the important contributions of the hidden curriculum, religious education and extra-curricular activities – in fact, the whole curriculum. This document can help individual teachers and whole schools identify and monitor across the curriculum the opportunities for preparing their students to be effective citizens of tomorrow's world.

Teacher Training

Education for international understanding, co-operation and peace, and education relating to human rights and fundamental freedoms are unlikely to develop spontaneously in schools. That is why it is very important for teacher education institutions that train new teachers and undertake in-service education to become strongly involved in 'international education'. This involves giving knowledge (the content) ... but ... knowledge is not enough. Much more important are the attitudes

and commitment developed in teachers: attitudes favourable to values that underlie international understanding and commitment to taking action to support peace, human rights
and fundamental freedoms'

(Pendoza-Florez, 1984).

Teachers cannot be expected to be experts on all the current issues on
which their students will want to be informed. Part of their training, therefore, needs to be in how to discover and use what resources are available.
Recent research in Wales (Hopkins 1990) found that more than 77 per cent
of teachers in training wanted to make their teaching more international. A
wide selection of excellent teaching material is available, and many voluntary organisations offer a range of other support to schools. Teachers can
find out more about what is available – through, for example, the development education centres listed by the National Association for Development
Education Centres (NADEC); the catalogues of Oxfam and Worldaware;
and the Council for Education in World Citizenship (CEWC).

Controversial Issues

Teachers are often chary about joining organisations whose main purpose
is to be a pressure group. However, the danger of campaigning or even
indoctrinating the students must not mean that controversial issues are
avoided. 'Education for Citizenship involves discussing controversial
issues upon which there is no clear consensus' (*Curriculum Guidance 8*).
An important part of the teacher's responsibility is to help the students
learn how, first, to understand and, then, to make up their own minds on
such issues.

Educating for World Citizenship – Some Practical Suggestions

In order to be able to make the decisions of responsible citizenship, people
need accurate and up-to-date knowledge as well as the skill of knowing
how to find appropriate information in the future. Students need practice in
effectively using newspapers, broadcasts, libraries and the information put
out by pressure groups and other organisations.

But information is not enough. We have to bring it alive and make it relevant for the students. Role play, simulations and games can bring fun,
involvement and insight into issues. Conferences and workshops can offer
new and stimulating contacts. Students' involvement in planning and
organisation gives useful experience and increased commitment.

Linking and exchanges have much potential but they need to be undertaken with care. The UK One World Linking Association (UKOWLA)
offers advice and support, particularly for links with economically
deprived countries. Not only can links be with schools, colleges or communities; they can also be with overseas development projects – such as those
offered by the Co-Action programme, administered by CEWC. Service,

too, offers a chance for direct involvement in issues – which can have an international dimension.

There are many other innovative ways of strengthening the international dimension of the curriculum. These can be in the classroom, in assemblies, in special events or in extra-curricular activities. They include involvement in exhibitions, competitions, award schemes, current events (such as Central America Week or Human Rights Day), development of new resources, and research projects on education for international citizenship. There are multicultural and international theatre, music and arts programmes on offer to schools and colleges.

Conclusions

As the Society of Education Officers and the Local Government International Bureau said recently:

> All sectors and organisations are being urged to think internationally in preparation for the Single European Market. It is important, however, that we avoid the dangers of an inward-looking Europe – and here we must look for every opportunity to widen perceptions of citizenship in a global context and to explore the various international implications of these and other changes in the European scene, particularly for developing countries in the Third World.
>
> (1989)

Such opportunities exist in abundance at all levels of education. They occur in specific topics in every subject of the curriculum and cross-curricular themes.

However, there is a danger that something that is everyone's job becomes no one's job. Careful monitoring is important. One way of doing this is to list the important topics, skills, processes and aspects of awareness that need to be covered, and to have a curriculum audit to ensure that they are. CEWC (1992) and the criteria for education for international understanding given in CEWC (1986) can be used as the basis for such monitoring. INSET workshops are available to cover this crucial activity.

It is not just some of our students who are going to have international rights and responsibilities: all are. All need to be aware of these and to have the necessary knowledge, attitudes, skills and understanding to take on the international 'opportunities, responsibilities and experiences of adult life' (Education Reform Act) for which their formal education has a responsibility to prepare them.

We have a crucial responsibility in preparing the citizens of tomorrow's world for these challenges and responsibilities. This preparation is an integral part of their education. As the Swann report said:

> A good education must...give every youngster the knowledge, understanding and skills to function effectively as an individual, as a citizen in a wider national society and in the world community of which he (or she) is also a member.'
>
> (DES, 1985)

118

References

Brandt, W. (1980) *North-South: A Programme for Survival* (The report of the independent commission on international development issues under the chairmanship of Willy Brandt). London: Pan Books.

CEWC (1986) *Citizens of the World*. London: CEWC.

CEWC (1992) *World Dimensions in the National Curriculum: A Guide to the International Curriculum* (available from CEWC).

DES (1977) *Education in Schools: A Consultative Document*. London: HMSO Cmnd 6869.

DES (1985) *Education for All* (The Swann Report). London: HMSO.

Hopkins, A. (1990) *Development Education and Teacher Education in Wales*. Cardiff: University of Wales College.

Pendoza-Florez, A. (1984) 'Implications for Teacher Education: the content' *Teaching for International Understanding, Peace and Human Rights*. London: UNESCO.

Society of Education Officers (1989) *Promoting International Perspectives in Curriculum Policy*. Local Government International Bureau.

Speaker's Commission (1990) *Encouraging Citizenship: Report of the Speaker's Commission on Citizenship*. London: HMSO.

UNICEF (1992) *State of the World's Children*. London: UNICEF.

United Nations Information Department (1985) *Universal Declaration of Human Rights* (available from CEWC).

World Development Movement (1991) 'Labour gears up on aid', in *Spur*, April.

ORGANISATIONS

Central America Week, 82 Margaret Street, London W1N 8LH

CEWC, Seymour Mews House, Seymour Mews, London W1H 9PE; 071 935 1752

NADEC, 6 Endsleigh Street, London WC1H 0DX; 071 388 2670

Oxfam, 274 Banbury Road, Oxford OX2 7DZ; 0865 311311

UKOWLA, c/o Mary Stead, Town Hall, Rose Hill, Chesterfield S40 1LP; 0246 216320

Worldaware (formerly Centre for World Development Education), 1 Catton Street, London WC1R 4AB; 071 831 3844

LAW-RELATED EDUCATION

Don Rowe

Fundamentally, the status of citizenship is based upon the legal relationship between the individual and the state. Education for citizenship must therefore provide the knowledge and understanding necessary for individuals to claim their rights as citizens and to exercise their appropriate duties. These rights and duties are to a large extent enshrined in the law, which represents the common code of conduct binding on all citizens. In practice, individuals subscribe to a number of different moral codes, emanating from, for example, their families or their cultural or religous backgrounds. Most of these value-centred communities take very great care to induct their young people into the rules and values of membership. Yet it is remarkable that society as a whole has very largely neglected to set out for its young people what the role of citizen entails.

Traditionally, citizenship per se has not featured prominently in the curriculum of British schools for a number of reasons, not the least being that the law itself is highly complex and has been regarded as hard to teach to all but the most able. In recent years, a number of factors have raised public awareness of the importance of knowing one's legal rights and duties. Ignorance breeds lack of confidence, disempowerment and social injustice. People who are ignorant of their rights are little better off than those who have no rights. This can foster alienation and reduce the inclination to act in a pro-social way through accepted democratic channels. Many young people feel this sense of powerlessness very acutely and this often seems to result in anti-social and law-breaking behaviour.

During the late 1970s and early 1980s, long before the publication of the National Curriculum Council's guidance on citizenship, there was a growing recognition that legal awareness should form part of the whole curriculum (e.g. HMI, 1977; David, 1983). Following an offer of sponsorship from the Law Society, the School Curriculum Development Committee initiated the Law in Education (14–16) Project which began work in 1984 to develop a pedagogy for the teaching of law to students of a wide ability range by teachers who themselves were not legal experts, but fellow citizens. Working with teachers, lawyers and police officers from around the country, the project developed a model characterised by:

(a) an issues-based approach, drawing on a wide range of law-related situations and problems relevant to the needs and experiences of young citizens;
(b) the use of active learning methods to engage pupils at their own level and to encourage a sense of personal involvement and 'ownership' of the issues;
(c) a concept-based approach, designed to raise understanding of key

ideas (such as law, justice, rights) and basic legal principles (such as contract or negligence) without undue concentration on the complexities of case law;

(d) the development of legal and moral reasoning skills, with an emphasis on the importance of justice in public affairs, so that students develop skills of bringing the law under critical review;

(e) an emphasis on respect for other peoples' views and for democratic and non-violent means of resolving conflicts.

This 'legal awareness' model aims to equip future citizens with sufficient knowledge and skills to discover and use the law effectively, and the confidence and competence to participate in public life and the democratic processes. The approach is also characterised by an emphasis that all students are entitled to know and understand the law whereas, formerly, school-based law courses were all but confined to an academic elite (and even then in only 10 per cent of schools).

Despite the novelty of this approach in the UK, law-related education had become a well-established branch of social studies in the United States of America and was also taking root in the education systems of Canada, Australia, New Zealand and Southern Africa. Indeed, in the United States, it had become the fastest growing area of the social sciences by the mid 1980s.

The evaluation of the Law in Education Project materials (Rowe and Thorpe, 1989) indicated that, despite the inexperience of staff, teachers and pupils of all abilities regarded learning about the law as interesting, worthwhile and useful. Teachers saw its value as empowering pupils to understand and exercise their rights and duties at the same time as providing intellectual rigour. A poll of 167 pupils indicated that whilst 82 per cent of pupils said they had enjoyed the lessons, they were almost unanimous (99 per cent) in expressing the view that it was worthwhile and useful to understand the law. The use of open-ended discussion questions seemed able to engage the interest of, on the one hand, non-examination groups in comprehensive schools and, on the other, high flying academic groups. Some teachers reported surprisingly high levels of interest and debate from pupils who generally showed little interest in other school subjects (Rowe, 1988).

The Law Project had begun work on upper secondary materials because a MORI (1980) poll showed that this was where schools urgently felt the need for such materials. However, there was a clear need to enable teachers to address similar issues for lower age groups. With the advent of the National Curriculum and the identification of citizenship as an all-phase, cross-curricular theme, the Law in Education (11–14) Project was established under the aegis of the newly formed Citizenship Foundation. With a new grant from the National Curriculum Council and continuing support from the Law Society, new materials were developed for Key Stage 3 (Rowe and Thorpe, 1993). Although there is less of an emphasis on statute law, and the issues and case studies are less complex, there is no shortage of relevant material on which to draw. Issues addressed include, for example, the making of rules and laws, the role of the police, the morality of theft, and a number of social issues such as children's rights and environmental protection. These and other issues are used to develop understanding of the central concepts of rights, responsibilities, and justice.

Law-related education presents significant challenges to teachers, particularly when developing curricula for younger pupils. Traditionally, citizenship education has been regarded as more appropriate for secondary pupils. Nevertheless, it is clear that an awareness of rules and laws develops during the primary years as do concerns relating to rights, responsibilities and justice (Cullingford, 1992). However, in planning a coherent and continuous citizenship curriculum, primary teachers should avoid the temptation of falling back on a paternalistic model of citizenship in which pupils are not encouraged to engage in reflective enquiry but are expected instead to accept uncritically the status quo (e.g. with regard to school rules and practices). Primary pupils are well able to identify what they see as unfair. If they are not given the chance to discuss such issues in a helpful and constructive environment, many opportunities will be lost for the development of more constructive and mature attitudes.

Accordingly, the Citizenship Foundation is developing new materials for use in Key Stages 1 and 2 focusing on pupils' experiences of rules and laws, rights, responsibilities and justice. Hitherto, many primary schools have seen citizenship education mainly as a function of the hidden curriculum. Principally through the medium of story (but also using games and exercises) the materials raise issues of concern to primary age pupils, enabling teachers to bring out into the open, for consideration and review, problematic areas relating to the nature of living in community. Citizenship issues rarely present pupils with simple choices between right and wrong. Choices can be highly complex and intellectually demanding. When moral choices are made, individuals call upon a widening range of 'spheres of consideration' (beginning with self-interest, then taking in the interests of others and then the interests of the wider community). At the same time, the reasoning processes draw on increasingly abstract notions, to do with general moral principles. The wider the range of concerns, the more adequate will be the grounds on which the decision is made. Kohlberg's work has clearly demonstrated that pupils broaden their moral horizons through discussion of issues in which their own views are challenged by those drawn from a slightly wider sphere of consideration (see e.g. Blatt and Kohlberg, 1975).

The Primary Citizenship project also draws on the work of Matthew Lipman, the American philosopher, who has shown that primary children readily engage in philosophical enquiry (Lipman, 1980). Lipman's approaches employ stories as starters for the discussion of issues of concern to the group in a mutually supportive and respectful atmosphere.

122

The model of citizenship education which is based simply on laying down a framework of rules and laws (or rights and wrongs) and enforcing this with a range of sanctions may be successful in controlling behaviour but is unlikely to promote moral growth in the longer term because it provides no opportunites for pupils to understand and internalise such codes. Law-related citizenship education aims to help pupils understand the reasons for rules and laws and therefore more effectively to internalise them, so that they become increasingly autonomous in the moral sense.

Law-related education is now contributing significantly to the personal and social education of many secondary schools and is being nurtured lower down the age range. Its potential contribution to the whole curriculum and to the moral, cultural, and political education of pupils is clear and has been acknowledged by educators and politicians from across the political spectrum. It is imperative and right that citizens should know their rights and duties and that those in power should be accountable to an educated and informed citizenry. This can only be healthy for the future of democracy and for the protection of human rights.

References

Blatt, M. and Kohlberg, L. (1975) 'The effects of classroom moral discussion upon children's level of moral judgement,' *Journal of Moral Education*, **4** (2), 129–161.

Cullingford, C. (1992) *Children and Society – Children's Attitudes to Politics and Power*. London: Cassell.

David, K. (1983) *Personal and Social Education in Secondary Schools: report of the Schools Council working party on personal and social education*. London: Schools Council.

H.M.I. (1977) *Curriculum 11–16*. London: HMSO.

Lipman, M., Sharp, A.M. and Osanyan, F.S. (1980) *Philosophy in the Classroom* (2nd ed). Philadelphia: Temple University Press.

MORI (1980) *The Teaching of Law-Related Studies in Secondary Schools*. Research conducted for the Law Society. London: Law Society.

Rowe, D. (1988) *Evaluation Report of the Law in Education Project* (available from The Citizenship Foundation).

Rowe, D. and Thorpe, T. (1989) *Understand the Law: Vols 1–4*. London: Hodder and Stoughton.

Rowe, D and Thorpe, T. (1993) *Living with the Law: Vols 1–3*. London: Hodder and Stoughton.

COMMUNICATION AND MEDIA STUDIES

Adrian Stokes

If citizenship refers to the way we formalise the relationship between the individual and the group (family, institution, community, nation), it is the media which provide us with representations of that relationship. The importance of media education for education for citizenship lies in the extent to which such representations are themselves formative rather than simply reflective.

The individual who needs to acquire and understand 'essential information' with respect to citizenship (as stressed by *Curriculum Guidance* 8) also needs to understand how all such information is mediated. Additionally, in order to participate – to act on the basis of this 'essential information' – all citizens require a level of proficiency in communication which includes familiarity with a range of media. Without this combination of skill, understanding and 'essential information' the laudable objective of an 'active citizenship' characterised by 'independence of thought on social and moral issues' and participation in society on the basis of 'a personal moral code' (*Curriculum Guidance 8*, p.4) will remain an empty exhortation.

To present education for citizenship as needing media education is, however, something of a tautology since the current interest in the study of the media owes its origin to debates about the relationship between education and citizenship which predate the introduction of the National Curriculum by half a century. A dominant view saw education as a vital intervention between the individual and a debased and debasing mass culture:

> We cannot, as we might in a healthy state of culture, leave the citizen to be formed unconsciously by his environment; if anything like a worthy idea of satisfactory living is to be saved, he must be trained to discriminate and to resist.
>
> (Leavis and Thompson, 1933, p.5)

For Leavis, of course, it was the training in 'taste' and 'sensibility' offered by a 'literary education' that might enable the citizen to resist the 'multitudinous counterinfluences' of films, newspapers and advertising. Indeed many elements of the 'inoculation' approach to media education linger in the statutory orders for National Curriculum English where 'non-literary and media texts' (an invariable association) are to be scrutinised for their capacity to 'regulate', 'persuade' and 'reassure'.

Of course, education about the media has been through many revisions over recent decades and for some time now has enjoyed independent subject status at GCSE level (and more recently at A level) as 'Media Studies'. Whether or not Media Studies will survive as a subject additional to the basic Key Stage 4 curriculum is still a matter for lobbying and debate. Many media education campaigners are therefore relieved, and with good reason, to have some statutory toe-hold in the national curriculum through inscription within the orders for a 'core' subject, English, while at the same time having considerable reservations about the approach these orders imply.

Outside English, references to the media are scattered through NCC documents in a random fashion – cropping up in all the foundation subjects as well as the cross-curricular dimensions, themes and skills. In a sense, the cross-curricular relevance of the topic is advantageous and provides encouragement for media-related work which could make a strong contribution to education for citizenship. Unfortunately, though not surprisingly given the circumstances of the various working groups, there is no pattern to the expectations of pupils, in terms of Key Stage and Attainment Level, with respect to media-related activities. If media education is to make its vital contribution to education for citizenship, it cannot do so on the basis of its current status and definition within the national curriculum.

It is not difficult, however, looking beyond the prescribed curriculum, to find work in media education which encourages the development of skill and understanding in a manner closely reflecting the approach of *Curriculum Guidance 8*. The Education Department of the British Film Institute (BFI) has probably been the most important organisation in lobbying for and encouraging by example (at the political and curriculum levels respectively) more coherent approaches to media education. Two curriculum statements (primary and secondary, British Film Institute 1989, 1991) have successfully related curriculum organisation and classroom practice within a framework of key concepts (media agencies, media categories, media technologies, media languages, media audiences and media representations).

Generally consistent with this framework has been another and rather more directly formative influence on teachers – the GCSE syllabuses in Media Studies. In addition to providing guidance on conceptual frameworks for study, these syllabuses include, among the assessment objectives, the use of 'relevant practical skills'. Such skills may well be developed in preparation for a variety of written assignments, but some practical assignments or project work (a media production and an accompanying production log) are themselves specifically required by all syllabuses.

These key aspects of media education – analysis based on a conceptual framework and demonstration of practical media skills – correspond at several points to the approach to education for citizenship presented in *Curriculum Guidance 8*. 'Communication skills' are among the cross-curricular skills identified as 'objectives' of education for citizenship (p.3). While it is easy to stress the importance of communication skills, it is rather more difficult to devise and implement an approach for their systematic development across the curriculum. In this respect, they stand as a utilitarian re-casting of 'language across the curriculum' – extended to include modes of communication beyond the linguistic. Of course, English has been, and continues to be in populist political exhortations, identifiable as the key provider of skills in speaking, listening, reading and writing. Identifying a corresponding provider for a broader conception of skill in communication is rather more difficult. And yet *Curriculum Guidance 8* clearly, and quite rightly, expects pupils to become skilled in the use of a range of media. In Appendix 2 activities are proposed, across the Key Stages, which require pupils to deploy skills in a range of media – perhaps the clearest examples being at the reporting stage of an investigation: 'They present their findings in the form of a report, media presentation or other suitable form' (KS4).

Such examples, and there are many more in *Curriculum Guidance 8*, indicate some of the productive links that can be made between a key 'component' of education for citizenship and practical work in Media Studies at Key Stage 4. The suggestions quoted could hardly be said, however, to reflect a coherent conceptual basis for practical work (what is a report if not a form of media presentation?) From a crudely instrumental point of view this might not seem particularly significant, but it is important to set the development of practical skills in the full context of active citizenship. *Curriculum Guidance 8* makes explicit reference, for example, to the formative role of the media with respect to pupils' 'values, beliefs and moral codes' (p.4) and to pupils' understanding of 'the nature of family life' (p.7). More frequently, however, references to the media focus on a particular component of essential information without acknowledging the need for critical awareness of media processes: e.g. pupils investigate public services 'using written and visual sources' (p.23); 'pupils discuss human rights issues arising from newspaper articles and other media presentations' (p.24). What is left implicit in such references is how pupils will use the sources and how an issue arises from a particular presentation. If these questions are ignored, it is impossible for pupils to make the sort of independent and personal decisions advocated as part of active citizenship.

Suggesting that additional subjects, particularly at KS4, can contribute to education for citizenship, and citing Social Science as an example, *Curriculum Guidance 8* acknowledges the value of 'a conceptual framework within which education for citizenship may flourish' (p.14). Clearly, GCSE Media Studies provides just such a framework, with the advantage that it integrates the development of practical skills with the acquisition of knowledge and understanding. But it can hardly be satisfactory to limit the contribution of a conceptual framework to the hazardous and uncertain margins of KS4.

If all pupils are to benefit fully from education for citizenship throughout their schooling, the contribution of media education is indispensable. Despite the best efforts of the BFI and others, drawing on plentiful examples of current practice in primary and secondary schools, a coherent framework has not as yet been incorporated in the NCC's guidelines for the whole curriculum. For the majority of pupils, we are left with the limited

126

inscription of media education within English. The signs are that, far from an expansion, this is itself an element that is at risk in the current 'back to basics' revision of the English orders – a revision which, ironically enough, derives its justification from popular concern, fuelled by the media, over the standards of literacy of future citizens.

References

BFI (1989) *Primary Media Education: A Curriculum Statement*. London: British Film Institute.

BFI (1991) *Secondary Media Education: A Curriculum Statement*. London: British Film Institute.

Leavis, F.R. and Thompson, D. (1933) *Culture and Environment*. London: Chatto and Windus.

RECORDS OF ACHIEVEMENT

Gordon Vincent

Any meaningful programme of Education for Citizenship in a school requires more than the identification of relevant knowledge and skills in the National Curriculum programmes of study. Education for Citizenship is as much concerned with the quality of relationship in a school, the respect for individuals and perceptions of justice, equality, rights and responsibilities based on shared values. The education of pupils into these ideals requires the provision of a supportive school ethos. The development of positive attitudes about self and others comes through the experience of teamwork, negotiation, decision-making and the exercise of responsibilities. Increasingly, schools are providing a range of opportunities for experiential learning both in and out of school, for example work experience, residential fieldwork, outdoor activities, community service and charity work. These programmes and democratic procedures in schools, contribute to 'the intangibles which come from the spirit and ethos of each school, its pupils and its staff' (NCC, 1990f)

However, schools are today operating in a political climate which attaches great importance to the assessment of learning. In an observation on the DES consultation document, *The National Curriculum 5–16* (DES, 1987), Aldrich (1988) concluded that it was 'essentially concerned with testing, and that the test of core and foundation subjects is simply designed to facilitate that testing'. Yet the same consultative paper also gave a commitment to Records of Achievement as having an 'important role in recording performance and profiling a pupil's achievements across and beyond the National Curriculum'. A statutory assessment scheme to reinforce a prescribed National Curriculum, formal assessment techniques as a means of raising the standards of teaching, and the assessment of performance of pupils and schools as an instrument of accountability, are barely compatible with Records of Achievement. The latter is concerned with acknowledging individual worth, developing self-awarenes and motivation, recording a wide range of achievements and experiences, and providing a 'more rounded picture' (DES, 1984) of pupils. Clearly, Records of Achievement, with their emphasis on experiential learning, negotiation, review and descriptions of achievements, can encompass the less tangible areas of education for citizenship.

Nevertheless there needs to be an awareness of the issues which arise, if the skills and knowledge elements of citizenship being assessed through statutory instruments and the more intangible aspects are reported through Records of Achievement. Increasingly there is an extrinsic value attached to those elements of the curriculum which can be measured and recorded; they acquire status through their prominence in the statutory reporting procedures. Elements of the curriculum which are more difficult to test in an apparently objective manner, particularly those concerned with the processes of learning, are given less prominence.

There is a respectable literature on the history, design, and operation of Records of Achievement and the purpose of this brief paper is not to advocate their use in education for citizenship. However, there is a need to tackle the issue of quality assurance in Records of Achievement. For, if the intangibles in the current concept of education for citizenship are to acquire equal status with the skills and knowledge components in their recording and reporting, then the methodology will need to have rigour and public confidence.

Work with a group of Local Education Authorities in southern England (Southern Partnership for the Accreditation of Records of Achievement – SPARA) has demonstrated how the establishment of a Local Validation panel and external accreditation can help establish confidence and rigour in Records of Achievement. The first task is to establish a set of principles to which all subscribe. This can be obtained from the literature but it needs to be debated and internalised in each school. Such principles are likely to include: the recognition of achievements and experiences across and beyond the curriculum; the integration of assessment with teaching and learning; the involvement of pupils in reflection on and review of their progress; the identification of strengths, weaknesses and targets; the placing of achievements in context; being positive; avoiding sex-stereotyping and cultural bias; encouraging the participation of parents and other adults; recording only statements which can be authenticated.

Having agreed on the principles, and developed a procedure for recording and reporting achievement which leads to the production of a summative Record of Achievement, then it is necessary to monitor the extent to which the process satisfies the criteria established. This has to be undertaken in such a way as to give credibility and currency to the statements about pupils in the Records of Achievement. The process leading to the production of a Record of Achievement must be subject to examination by both the teachers and other adults with an interest. A Local Validation Panel can be formed to undertake this task on behalf of the school and might consist of a representative from the governing body, the staff, the careers service, a local company and a higher education institution, for example.

The Local Validation Panel is not concerned with assessing the quality of the teaching nor the attainment of the students. The panel's task is to satisfy itself that the process and procedures leading to the issuing of a Record of Achievement, reflect the principles agreed. The panel members are therefore required to talk to pupils and staff involved and to observe aspects of their practice. Not all members of the Local Validation Panel will be teachers and it is therefore important to translate the principles into a set of questions for laypersons which will assist them in identifying issues. For example, pupils might be asked how often there had been an opportunity to discuss progress with a teacher; the teacher could be asked what opportunities there were for reviewing progress with a pupil; while the school's senior management could explain the arrangements made for one-to-one discussions between teachers and pupils. SPARA has successfully developed a set of lay questions to cover all of its principles and their application is a prerequisite for the accreditation of a school's Record of Achievement.

Mechanisms such as Local Validation will help to ensure that a pupil's progress in the more intangible areas of Education for citizenship are recorded and reported in a manner which is sympathetic to the ideals of a citizenship programme while not lacking in rigour or credibility. Records of Achievement and education for citizenship are compatible but it is important for both that there is an element of quality assurance.

References

Aldrich, R. (1988) 'The National Curriculum, an historical perspective,' in Lawton, D. and Chitty, C. (eds), *The National Curriculum*, Bedford Way Papers 33, University of London Institute of Education.

Department of Education and Science (1984) *Records of Achievement – A Statement of Policy*. London: HMSO.

Department of Education and Science (1987) *The National Curriculum 5–16: a consultative document*. London: HMSO.

SPARA document available from the author at Education Department, County Hall, Aylesbury, Bucks, HP20 1UZ. 0296 395000.

Index

H